ANGER

MANAGEMENT

WORKBOOK

A Self Help Guide for Men and for Women to Take Control and Master Your Emotions. Overcome Anger, Anxiety and Change Your Pattern of Relationships

Published By

Travis Cooper

Table of Contents

Introduction

Everyone understands the meaning of angry emotion and have experienced it—either as a full-fledged rage or as a fleeting annoyance.

This kind of emotion is entirely normal and is often a healthy emotion. However, when anger is out of control and turns destructive, anger can cause challenges—issues in your relationships, issues in your general quality of lifestyle, and problems at work. This guidebook is meant to assist you in managing and understanding this emotion.

Your feelings are important to your capability to cope with the difficulties of your life. When you are feeling good, you will be able to shrug off the most difficult of tasks ahead of you—but when you are in a miserable mood, you view the enjoyable task with a sense of doom and gloom. Hence, the need arises to recognize your emotions and identify their triggers and ways to manage them. Emotions such as anger and anxiety, when left unchecked, can be very dangerous and can hurt your inner self without being noticed.

Emotions also affect your relationship with other people around you. When an ally shares a tragic experience with you, and you respond by snickering instead of looking concerned or sad, you will seem to be insensitive and rude.

This workbook helps you to recognize and understand your emotions, and it explains why they are, at times, very strong. The workbook offers some practical ideas and techniques about how you can manage your emotions so that you can apply and harness them without allowing them to take control.

Chapter 1

Recognizing Your Emotion

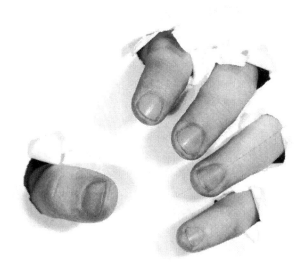

What Is Anger?

Anger is a normal emotion and often an automatic reaction to the pain of one type or another—whether emotional or physical. It can happen when someone feels threatened, do not feel well, experience some loss, or feel rejected.

The kind of pain that a person feels does not matter. What is critical is that the aspect of pain felt is unpleasant—and since angry emotions never happen in isolation but are followed by feelings of pain, anger is usually manifested as a secondhand feeling.

Pain by itself is not enough to cause angry emotions. It happens when the feeling of pain is coupled with anger-stimulating thoughts.

Examples of thoughts that can stimulate angry emotions include interpretations, evaluation, assumptions, or personal assessments of events that get people to think that another person is trying to harm them—this can be either consciously or not.

At this point, anger will be assumed as a social feeling—you often have a victim that your angry emotions are directed towards (remember that this victim can also be yourself). Emotions of pain, coupled with anger stimulating thoughts, prompt a person to take a particular response, face the danger, and protect themselves by striking out against the victim they think is harming or causing them pain.

Anger as a Substitute Emotion

Sometimes, most people get themselves to be upset so that they do not have to feel any pain. Most people alter their emotions of pain into angry emotions because it feels better to be angry than to be in pain. The alteration of pain into angry emotions may be done unconsciously or consciously.

Being in an angry state rather than in pain has some merits—mainly among the merits is a distraction. Primarily, those who are feeling pain think about their painful experiences. However, people who are angry do bare thoughts of causing harm to people who have caused pain to them. An aspect of the transmutation of pain into anger includes an attention shift from one's self to another.

Anger provides a perfect smokescreen for the feeling of vulnerability—when you become angry, it builds a feeling of moral superiority, power, and righteousness that is not there when you are in pain. When you have angry emotions, you are upset with a cause. A popular refrain is, "The person who has hurt me is wrong—he or she should be punished accordingly." It's sporadic that you will get upset with another person that has not hurt you in a significant manner.

Defining Anger

The definition of whether a person's anger is an issue usually changes to whether or not another person does consent with them that the angry response they manifest in the name of anger is justifiable.

People who are angry usually feel that their angry response is justified. However, some people do not usually consent to their response. The social judgment of anger brings an actual outcome for the angry person. An angry person will often feel justified in committing an aggressive reaction—but when a jury of peers or a judge does not view it in that manner, the person who is angry may still be sentenced. If a partner does not consent that anger was justified, a relationship may be in serious trouble.

Nature of Anger

It is a natural emotional condition that varies in intensity from severe irritation to a mild rage and fury. Just like other feelings, angry emotion is accompanied by physiological and biological alterations; when you are angry, your blood pressure and heart rate increases, also the level of energy hormones, noradrenaline, and adrenalin increases.

It can be triggered by internal and external situations. You could get angry at a particular person or a situation, or your angry emotions could be triggered by brooding or worrying about your challenges. Experiences of enraging or traumatic situations can also cause angry emotions.

Anger Expression

The natural, intuitive manner to show anger is to react aggressively. It is a natural, adaptive reaction to danger; anger motivates powerful, usually aggressive, behaviors, and feelings, that allows you to retaliate and to protect yourself when you are being hurt. A specific level of anger, therefore, is essential to your natural survival.

Contrary, you cannot physically react at every object or person that annoys or irritates you; social laws, common sense, and norms create limits on how far your angry emotions can take you.

Most people apply a range of both unconscious and conscious techniques to manage their angry emotions. The three main procedures are expressing, suppressing, and calming your angry emotions. How you express your anger is not in an aggressive way, but in an assertive way which is the healthiest manner to show your angry emotions. For you to achieve this assertive way, you have to learn and understand how to make clear what are your needs, and how to get your desires achieved, without harming anyone. Assertiveness does not mean being demanding or pushy; it means that you are respectful to yourself and those around you.

Feelings of being angry can be effectively suppressed, then redirected or converted. This occurs when you hold in your angry emotions, stop thinking about your anger, and concentrate on something positive in your life. The purpose is to suppress or inhibit your angry emotions and turn them into a constructive habit. The harm in this kind of reaction is that if it is not let outwardly, your angry emotions can turn inward on yourself. Anger that is turned inward may lead to depression, hypertension, or high blood pressure.

Recognizing Signs of Anger

You need to learn how to recognize your angry emotions before you get into the details of on the methods to manage your emotions. You require answers to questions like:

- How do my angry reactions affect other people?

- What things/places/events/people get me angry?

- How do I respond when I am angry?

- How do I get to know that I am angry?

Getting the response to these questions may take some time. It's likely that you will rattle off some triggers that make you angry. You might even identify some sings that you manifest when you are at your angry state. These fast responses are only the start, however—the low hanging apple. You will desire to constantly ask yourself the above questions for some time before you get satisfied that you are completely knowledgeable about your personal emotions of anger.

Recognizing Anger's Physiological Signs

The first step is to learn and understand how to recognize when you are angry. Most people who are angry view their feelings as a white and black state, they are either calm or raging mad. Anger is not white and black, but rather grey. Anger happens on a continuum between calm and rage where most people go through some gradation of angry emotions between the two extremes.

The same people who perceive anger in terms of extremes have challenges in recognizing when they are facing intermediate anger conditions. Luckily, some people face several emotional, behavioral, and physical cues that they apply to help them know when they are getting upset.

Emotionally, you may feel:

- Anxious

- Guilty

- Like striking out physically or verbally

- Resentful

- Depressed or sad

- Like getting away from the situation

- Irritated

Physical signs include:

- Trembling or shaking

- Dizziness

- Sweating particularly on your palms

- Feeling hot in the face or neck

- Headache

- Rapid and increased heart rate

- Grinding your teeth or jaw clenching

- Stomachache

You may also notice that you are:

- Raising your voice

- Starting to cry, scream or yell

- Acting in abrasive or abusive behavior

- Pacing

- Getting sarcastic

- Rubbing your head

- Cupping your fist with your other hand

How to Identify and Respond to Anger

Before you can learn and understand how to manage your angry emotions and your cognitive responses to feeling angry, you must first have the ability to identify when you are angry. Paying close attention, not only to your emotions but to the signs that your body is showing in terms of physiological signs of anger.

Recognizing Anger

Anger is not a major problem; anger is a natural, normal emotional reaction. It is how you handle and manage the emotion of anger that it gets to be a problem. Recognizing angry emotions is the first step in assisting a person who applies destructive methods or violence in dealing with anger to change the manner it makes them react. You can't change the way angry emotions makes you feel, but you can change how you react to the emotion.

The first early signs of angry emotions are physical tension, a pit on the stomach feeling, or a tight grip on the muscles. You might also feel a break out in sweat or cold. Your heart will beat abnormally, and your breathing pace may change. Often, you respond to these physical feelings before thinking about a rational reaction you would take. Some people may opt to shut down fully and internalize their angry emotions.

If you train yourself how to recognize the physical signs, you can teach your mind to manage your reaction; you can pause your overt response and give yourself time to think rationally. If you are prone to violence, you can recognize the physical symptoms as a cue to take a time out. When you tend to internalize your angry feelings, it can be an unhealthy way to manage your anger; you can apply the physical cues to assist you to recognize the importance to express your emotions outwardly.

When you have an issue with your anger; when you respond to angry emotions with self-destructive methods or violence, it will be important for you to carry out a self-assessment of anger in your life. These include:

Step One

Try and think about instances in your life you have seen on how to handle and control angry emotions. Did your guardian often overreact to issues that made him/her angry? Was your home a place of frustration and tension? What about other influential people in your life? Have you incorporated responses to angry emotions into your life from the different behaviors that you have seen? Was it okay or not okay to express angry emotions in your home? Did you have a voice?

Step Two

Try and think about events that seem to stimulate your angry emotions. Do particular things seem to set you off? Do you become upset when you feel ridiculed, teased, or rejected? So particular habits get you angry?

Step Three

Once you have identified what causes your anger, you will have the ability to work on figuring out rational alternatives. The old fashioned concept that angry

emotions should be fully expressed always, because it's not healthy to hold it inside, is not the truth. Often expressing your angry emotions, particularly if you have violent or negative means of expressing your emotion, can cause more violent expressions of anger as time goes by.

Oftentimes, when you repress, your anger is not good; this means that you are not handling the things that lead to your anger, so your angry emotions will keep on occurring. The perfect solution is to identify the factors that lead to your anger and get rid of them, if possible, or you can work through the factors that lead to a specific set of anger responses.

Action Versus Emotion

The most vital thing that you can perform when you are dealing with how to manage your anger is to recognize that the emotion you feel when you get angry, and your physical reaction to anger are separate aspects. You can unlearn the behavior of your response to angrily emotion, even when you can't fully get rid of the emotion of anger. You can learn and understand

16

better means of responding to angry emotions that are not as harmful to others and you.

Anger and Irrational Thoughts

Sometimes, even without realizing it, you become the target of your thought processes and develop an angry reaction, even when there is no actual need to get angry. Have you ever seen people who seem angry always? Mostly, anger has become the emotion that they are used to facing.

It is possible to alter your approach to the factors that lead to you being angry and to minimize the emotional reaction. Usually, your life experiences form a defense mechanism that causes you to apply anger as a means of protecting yourself, like a shield. Not only can you teach yourself to realize that what others say about you does not really influence who you are, but you can recognize that you may have developed an over-sensitive nature to this specific kind of event.

There is a possibility that you can have an expectation that things will go how you desire them to, and when they do not, you may have the behavior of getting angry. This may be a behavior that you have developed over some time. Perhaps it's the perfect time for you to retrain yourself to realize that, while it is okay to shape the universe that you desire, you are not often in control of the environment. You can only manage your preferences, not the preferences of other people. If you learn to let go and recognize irrational expectations, you can lessen your angry emotions.

It is very crucial for those who tend to repress their angry emotions in various means to understand that anger is simply a natural emotion; there is no big difference to the other emotions that they face. It is not bad or good; it is something to be dwelt or ignored upon. Anger is just another emotion that must be dealt with, and your aim must be learning how to handle anger in the most effective and healthy means possible. It is critical to learn and understand how to be assertive to protect yourself without being violent or reactionary.

When other people are the source of your angry emotions, it is because of how you perceive their habit towards you. You may have adopted an attitude that other people should not frustrate you, that you are entitled to live a life free of frustration. By altering your perception and realizing that life will give you challenges, even when you do not want the obstacles, you will be more ready for the obstacles when they come and less likely to overreact.

Chapter 2

Physiology of Anger

Just like any other natural emotions, angry emotions are experienced both in your body and your mind. There's a complex cycle of the body or physiological events that happen as you get angry.

Natural emotions, more or less, start inside a structure in your brain, which is called the amygdala. The amygdala is the part of your brain that is enabled to identify dangers to your well-being and to send out an alarm when the danger is identified, which then causes you to take necessary steps to defend yourself. Amygdala is very efficient at warning you of the dangers, that it gets you to react before the cortex checks on the reasonableness of your response. The cortex is the part of the brain that is enabled for judgment and thought process. Your brain is wired in a manner to make you react before you can efficiently consider the results of your responses. This is not an excuse for you to misbehave—people can manage their aggressive impulses, and you can, too, with several practices.

As you experience angry emotions, your body muscles tense up. In the brain, there are neurotransmitter called catecholamines that are triggered, making you experience a flush of emotional energy that lasts up to some minutes. The flush of energy is the one that leads to a common angry urge to take instant protective response. At the same time, your heart rate increases, blood pressure goes up, and breathing rate goes up. Your face may flush as the blood flow increases entering your extremities and limbs in readiness for a physical reaction. Your attention narrows and gets locked onto the victim of your angry emotions. In fast succession, additional brain hormones are stimulated that causes a lasting condition of arousal. You are now prepared to fight.

There is a possibility of your feelings to burst out of control, the prefrontal cortex of the brain, that is behind the forehead, is able to keep your emotions in proportion. When the amygdala is responsible for your emotions, the prefrontal cortex is responsible for judgment. The left prefrontal cortex can switch off your angry emotions. The left prefrontal cortex acts in an executive function to keep situations under control. Being in control over your emotions means learning techniques to assist your prefrontal cortex to get the upper hand over your amygdala so that you have total control over how you respond to angry emotions. Among the several techniques that make this possible are relaxation methods; reduces arousal and minimizes your amygdala functions and the application of cognitive control methods that assist you to practice applying your judgment to override your emotional responses.

When anger has a physiological preparation stage through which your resources are prepared for retaliation, it also has a wind-down stage. You begin to relax towards your resting condition when the victim of your anger is no longer an immediate threat to your emotions. It is very hard to relax from an angry condition. The adrenaline-caused arousal that happens during an angry response lasts a very long time, and reduces your anger threshold, making it easier for you to become angry again in the future. Though you calm down, it takes a very long time for you to get back to your resting condition. During this process, you are likely to become very upset in reaction to minor irritation that normally would not bother you.

The same arousal that keeps you ready for angrier emotion, it can also distract your capability to remember details of your angry outbursts. Arousal is very important for efficient recalling. As most student would understand, it is very hard to learn new material while sleepy. A moderate amount of arousal assists the brain in enhancing performance, focus, and memory. There is an optimum amount of arousal that benefits the memory, and when the arousal is above the optimal amount, arousal makes it very hard for new memories to be created. A large amount of arousal greatly minimizes your capability to focus. This is the reason as to why it is hard to recall details of very explosive arguments.

How Anger Occurs in Your Brain

Have you ever wondered what automatic coupling of normal neurological forces are functioning when you get angry? With the aim of your interaction being to find out how to improve dealing with your angry emotions, we shall look at how anger occurs in the brain.

Brain's Emotional Center

The cortex is the part responsible for thinking where judgment and logic reside. The cerebral cortex is the outer part of your brain that is divided into lobes. Just think of it as the strategy center system of your brain. The emotional centre of the brain is the limbic system. The limbic system is situated on the lower part of the brain, and it is considered to be more primitive than the cortex.

When you are expressing and experiencing anger, the thinking part of your brain is not operation, but generally, the limbic system of your brain is operation

Have You Encountered Amygdala Today?

In the limbic system of your brain is a small part known as the amygdala, the storehouse for emotional memories. This is also the part of your brain that is responsible for flight or fight responses, your natural survival instincts.

The data collected from the universe around you go via the amygdala where a decision is taken whether to pass the information to the limbic system or the cerebral cortex. When the incoming data stimulates enough emotional thoughts, the amygdala overrides the cerebral cortex, meaning that the data will be passed to the limbic system causing you to respond using the amygdala.

During the override process, the amygdala operates without much consideration of the outcome. This is because the amygdala is not responsible for evaluating, judging, or thinking. This reactive event is called the amygdala hijacking.

Getting Ready for the Hormones (Panic)

If the amygdala is hijacked, a large amount of hormones is stimulated and released, that lead to emotional and physical harm. A surge of emotional energy follows, getting you ready for the flight or fight reaction. The effect of this hormonal flush lasts for some minutes during which you are out of control and may do things or say things that you might regret later when the limbic system of the brain reengages.

Why, at Times, Does Counting to Ten Not Work?

When you have a long-lasting hormone in your body system, this explains why you had an initial, angry, robust response, then you seem to calm down, but later experience a huge flair-up that is disproportionate to the event, due to several small incidents happening while the hormone was active in your blood system.

On average, it takes up to twenty minutes for someone who has faced any angry state of arousal with calming down, to shift from the functioning, emotional part to the thinking part of the brain.

Many Things to Digest

Perhaps you require to be aware that a lot occurs in the physiological aspect when you get angry.

What is vital to know is:

- It will usually take about twenty minutes before you can once again become more logical.

- Anger includes a trigger to the emotions that easily charges up, causing to you lose it.

Knowing that could assist you as you handle and manage your angry emotions or someone's else angry emotions. When you know that someone's amygdala has been hijacked, then you should give them over twenty minutes before you try to discuss or resolve what occurred since it takes about twenty minutes for the hormonal released to minimize in intensity.

Recognizing and Managing Your Own Emotions

Why it is essential to understand one's feelings and at the same time understanding those emotions of other people. It is also essential for one to identify and understand their own emotions and why they are strong at some point if our life. You will get to learn ways in which you, as a person, can manage your own emotions for you to use them and harness them.

Before you start the process of recognizing and managing your feelings, you need to ask yourself the following two questions:

- How do you feel?

- How do you know?

As you are taking time to be aware of your feelings, also take time to be aware of other peoples' emotions.

How Do Other People Around You Feel, and How Do You Get to Know?

There are several ways in which you can tell how other people are feeling, this can be possible by you observing what they say and their behavior at that particular time, this is possible when you observe their body language. Most research has it that most of the human communication is non-verbal; this suggests that it comes from facial expression and body language.

The Brain and Emotions

Our emotions are unconsciously directed. The limbic system in our body is responsible for controlling and anything that deals with our emotions. This system in our brain has evolved in human history, making it quite primitive. This is an explanation as to why emotional response tends to be often straightforward, but also it is compelling. The responses are mainly based on the need to survive. Your emotions are linked to your memory and the experiences you have had in the past. This explains why your emotional stimulus to a previous experience tends to be active as compared to when the experience happened. Young ones feel emotions, but they can't necessarily reason out how they are feeling. This explains that our emotions are closely tied to our values: emotional response tells us when one of our key values has been challenged.

When you get to understand the linkage between your memory and your values, it is when you will be able to manage your emotional response. An emotional response does not necessarily be linked to your current situation, but one can overcome the emotional response with reasoning and be aware and mindful of your reactions.

Your journey towards mastering your emotions begins with knowing yourself in and out. The first step for building higher emotional intelligence is to plug in to own emotions. Only when we are aware of our emotions are we able to manage them more effectively. Being self-aware is the foundation of emotional intelligence. When we are self-aware, we can recognize our own emotions and be more in tune with them on a regular basis, thus identifying the thoughts and feelings driven by these emotions and the ability to regulate them optimally for the overall good in a situation.

Folks who are self-aware will rarely be controlled by their emotions because they know the potential responses or reactions certain emotions evoke and can control them more effectively when it happens. When we know how you think and feel, it is simpler to identify our complete emotional framework and avoid being a victim of our own damaging emotions. We hold absolute control over our responses in any situation and can steer even potential difficult situations in the right direction. This builds greater self-assurance and rewarding relationships.

Here are some of the best ways to master self-awareness:

I)   Journaling

Journaling is an incredibly effective way to develop a deeper understanding of our thoughts, feelings, and emotions at the start or end of each day or any point during the day. It is like mastering our emotions by taking stock of them just like you would for physical products.

Write precisely how you feel when some specific situation has happened during the day. Mention everything, including physiological reactions, emotions, sensations (more rapid heartbeat, increased sweating, feeling of dizziness, etc.), and so on.

Create a list of several roles that you play on a daily basis. For example, parent, spouse co-worker, manager, gym buddy, friend, etc. What are the feelings connected to every role you play at the end of the day?

For instance, you may be a happy parent but a stressed or frustrated professional. Likewise, you may be a fulfilled spouse but a nervous businessperson. From the first day of your journey towards greater emotional intelligence, think of each vital role and your emotions towards the role. When you recognize your feelings for each role, there is greater power in managing these emotions towards a particular role. It doesn't just boost understanding of your emotions towards the particular role but also puts you in control of the feelings and emotions experienced towards the relationship.

II) Doing a periodic mental check-in

Do what annoying yet well-intended house-keepers and guests' service people do in hotels. They keep knocking on the door and asking you if you require anything. Likewise, knock on your mental door without really asking, "Any cleaning services needed?" and plug into how you are feeling at any point. You do this several times a day. Take a comprehensive account of your feelings. Where are these emotions coming from? Why do you feel the way you do? What physical signs reveal these emotions? Do your feelings and emotions occur in rapid succession? Are they combined by physical sensations or physiological reactions? Are these emotions obvious through your body language (expressions, gestures, leg movements, postures)? Are your emotions easily observed by other people? Are your decisions driven by your emotions? Although it is near impossible, attempt to notice your feelings from a non-judgmental manner.

Learning to How to Manage Your Emotions

A person chooses how they want to feel. You cannot control other people's actions, but you can be able to control how you react to them. Most people get angry, which is an easy thing to do, but you being angry with the right person at the right time and at the right degree and with the right cause is one of the most difficult activity that human being finds it difficult to achieve. This not within every person's power and it is not easy.

Emotional Energy

High Positive energy. This kind of energy allows you to be at your best state, but one cannot be in this state forever. As time passes by, you need to reduce positive energy. You need to stay positive, and this will help you recover quickly. When you get yourself dipped into more negative feelings, you will feel the burning out sensation.

High Negative Energy

This can be quite an uncomfortable place you want to be as a person. You will always have the feeling that you are always fighting for survival all the time. This energy state will reach a point where you need to reduce the energy since the negative energy can lead to burning out when left to accumulate over some time.

Positive Actions That May Help You to Manage Your Emotions

There are some positive actions or exercises that one can take part in that may help them to manage their emotions more positively. You may try the following activities and see whether they will work for you:

Being Kind to Other People

By being kind to other people, you will be able to help yourself bet not worrying too much about yourself.

Physical Exercise

Daily exercises will help your body by releasing reward and pleasure chemicals such as the dopamine. This enzyme helps the body to be in a feel better state.

When a person is healthy, he/she can manage their emotions more positively.

Talking to Other People
Always enjoy being around people who you love. Spend time with them and enjoy their company.

Always Distracting Yourself
Some emotional response makes one feel very shallow. Distracting yourself will help you get your mind to think about other positive things rather than thinking of the negative event. For example, you can watch a bit of TV or surfing the internet, and this will probably help you forget that what is making you feel a bit down and shallow.

Being Open and Always Accepting What Is Going on in Your Life
Appreciating what you are going through in your life will help you avoid excessive criticism.

Never Giving in to Negative Thinking
When you find yourself being in negative thoughts, try as much as possible not to let the negative thought take control of your actions, Hence the need to find

evidence against the negative thoughts so as you can challenge them.

Always Being Grateful

Be the kind of person who always appreciates any deed that has been for you no matter how small it may seem. Away remember the deeds.

Spending Some Time Outside

Having fresh air for yourself, especially around nature, is very helpful for you since it calms your emotions.

Always Playing to Your Emotions

This means you should always do things that you enjoy and also things that are good for you.

Application of Reasoning to Emotion

The most important thing is that you should be aware of your emotional responses, also understanding what might be causing the emotional response. By doing so, you will be able to change how you are feeling. At this point, you may apply some reasoning to the situation and manage your emotions appropriately.

In this case, you may find it very essential for you to ask yourself some of the questions that are listed below:

- Is there any other person that you could ask about this situation who may help you out?

- Is the action that you are doing fit your values?

- If what you are doing is not okay. What else could you do that might fit you better?

- What are the effects of your action to you and the other people?

- What do you think you should do about the current situation?

- How do you feel in person about the current situation?

You will find out that these questions will apply reason to an emotional response before you react to any situation.

Decision-Making with Your Emotions

A person draws reason and emotion or a combination of logic and emotion when making decisions.

Emotional Decision

Emotions play a bigger role in times that we make mistakes; this is so that we may be aware of the emotions that we are experiencing. Most people may argue that decision making is solely based on logic. Best decisions are mostly made using both emotion and logic. When you only use one, your decision may either not be balanced or may not have satisfied your emotional needs. It is, therefore, important to combine more rational considerations with your emotional response.

Combining rational consideration with an emotional response can be achieved by doing the following key steps:

- Always think how you will feel as a consequence of each of your actions to a certain situation.

- Always pause or stop before deciding; this allows you to think first before you react to any situation.

- When you feel there is no hurry in making a decision, always take some time out before making the decision.

- Weigh your decisions against your values, check whether your decision fits perfectly to your values. If not, why not?

- You should always consider the consequence of your action and how your consequence will affect other people. Are you happy with the effects of your actions?

- Try and think about how someone who you respect would think about your decision. Would you be proud of your decision and it's an effect on you and other people around you?

- Lastly, you should think of the reputation if everyone would take similar action if it is a disaster, then there is no need for you to perform the action.

It is essential for you to be aware of your emotion and those of other people. People who have a high emotional intelligence level will always tend to think about others first before they react to any situation— they achieve this by them understanding and being aware of other people's emotion. You will learn that people will always forget what you said, they will always forget what you did to them, but they will never forget how you made them feel at a particular point in time.

Chapter 3

Types of Anger

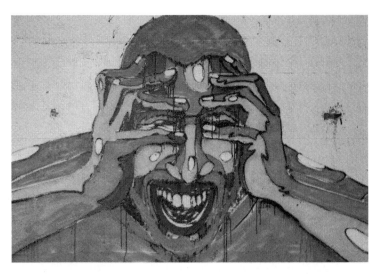

Anger is usually viewed as a major challenge in the modern universe. It can make you perform things that you would never think of yourself being able to do. The biggest challenge with anger is that in its severe form, anger seems to inhibit your self-control, leaving you almost helpless to stop yourself from performing something that you know you should not do. You become angry from time to time, and you usually have a good reason to be angry. That, in itself, is not something bad. It is not the presence of anger that leads to the problem—it is how you respond to the angry emotions building up inside you that will determine whether your anger is a problem or not.

The key to effective anger management is effective processing of the anger and converting it from something to be feared to a friend. As soon as you realize that you are becoming angry about a particular situation, you are able to choose a course of action that allows you to stay calm while handling the issue you are presented with. To be able to identify your anger, it lies in being able to identify the kind of anger you experience. There are several types of anger, and each one of them can cause you to respond in a different way.

This should assist you in determining which anger type you experience the most. This is the first step to manage your anger.

Chronic Anger

This is a type of anger that is ongoing, resentment towards others, frustration to specific circumstances, and angry emotions towards self. Chronic anger is characterized by constant irritation; a prolonged nature of this kind of anger can profoundly adverse effects on one's wellbeing and health.

People who experience this type of anger are those who hate the universe—they hate every person in the universe, hate themselves, and often cannot explain why. People with this type of anger are those people whom you will assume are going to get angry if you interact with them. Perhaps unfairly, you do not wait for them to become angry; you begin to get ready for an outburst or an explosion.

Management Strategy

Often spend more time reflecting on the root causes of your anger emotion. If you are able to identify the source of your upset and resentment, you may be able to resolve the inner feud you are facing by forgiving yourself and other people for the past transgressions.

The forgiveness process is very powerful and can assist in resolving your well-being and health.

Volatile Anger

If this is the type of anger you experience, you are very fast to get angry about perceived annoyance, both small and big. Once you have impulsively expressed your angry emotions, you usually calm down just as fast.

When something is volatile, it is explosive. In this case, anger behaves in a similar manner. Volatile anger can explode out of nowhere and can be very violent.

Volatile anger usually comes and goes with no warning. The main issue with this type of anger is that it does not require a reason, and therefore, it is very hard to predict.

Management Strategy

Often identify the physical symptoms and signs that precede a volatile outburst, and apply relaxation tactics to stop your anger from escalating. Using the deep breathing technique.

Self-Inflicted Anger

Most people apply self-inflicted anger to punish themselves for thinking they have done something wrong.

The perfect remedy for a short temper is a long walk.

Management Strategy

You should know about cognitive reframing techniques. This is a method that involves identifying then disputing maladaptive or irrational thoughts. Reframing is a way of experiencing and viewing events, emotions, concepts, and ideas to figure out more positive options. In the aspect of cognitive therapy, cognitive reframing is called cognitive restructuring.

Apply the reframing methods to transform and to challenge any self-defeating feelings and thoughts that you are facing. Mindfulness meditation can assist to focus you in the current moment and deal with any impulses to engage in self-harming habits.

Retaliatory Anger

This the most popular kind of anger, it happens as a direct reaction to another person doing something that makes you angry or lashes out at you.

Rather than attempting to resolve the problem effectively, you deem it necessary to even the score. You are not prepared to let another person have the upper hand against you. You desire to prove a point and stop the other person from treating you harshly, so you improve your game and make sure that you gain the upper hand.

Management Strategy

Whether your desire is intentional or impulsive, it is vital to pause and think before you respond to it. Will your angry response enhance the event, or it will just worsen tie? By picking to diffuse the imminent feud, you will be able to avoid the unwanted long term outcome of revenge.

Verbal Anger

Anger that is expressed verbally and not physically. Stones and sticks may break your bones, but names will not hurt you. A verbal attack will not leave physical scars, but the emotional pain it causes can be very overwhelming.

Those who face this kind of anger apply criticism and insults to hurt people and to put them down psychologically. They intend to harm, and the choice of words is deliberately emotive and usually evokes imagery.

This type of anger is usually applied as a way of control where the angry person strips away the other person's self-esteem and will power. Once they have broken the person down, they can manipulate them to meet their needs.

Anger only dwells in the bosom of a fool.

Passive Anger

Most people use mockery and sarcasm as a means to express their angry emotions and keep away from conflict and confrontations. Passive anger is also called passive-aggressive behavior. It seems to be more popular in recent days.

Passive anger happens when the person who is angry has an issue with another person but refuses to be open about it. Instead, he/she adopt a hostile attitude to the other person through a variety of measures.

Management Strategy

You should learn proper assertive communication skills and figure out your fear of confrontations applying the "What if?" Instances. By developing a capability to articulate your frustration and confidently experience a variety of fears, you are more likely to achieve your needs, both professional relationship and personal relationship.

Overwhelming Anger

This is an unchecked kind of anger. Overwhelming anger often happens when you feel that a circumstance or a situation is above your control, resulting in a feeling of frustration and hopelessness. It is more common when you have taken on much responsibility that has overthrown your normal capability to cope up with natural stress.

People who experience this type of anger are much wrapped up in their angry emotions that they cannot take it anymore. They have difficulties in expressing their concerns and anger, and instead, they bottle up it all. Ultimately, they cannot hold it anymore, and it has to come out.

They usually resort to physical violence or even destruction, causing harm to someone else or themselves.

Management Strategy

It is very important to reach out for assistance if you are facing this kind of anger. Allow friends and family and professional allies know why you require support, whether it is assistance with babysitting or a work project. By alleviating potential sources of stress, you will regain a sense of behavioral and emotional control again.

Judgmental Anger

People who face this type of anger have low self-esteem, and they express their angry emotions by putting others down in public in an effort to attempt to make themselves look perfect.

I had an ally who had this type of anger. She would never express her voice in anger, but she was often putting people down to make herself look perfect. Making other people feel small so that you feel big, often backfires.

Paranoid Anger

This is the type of anger that is completely without a cause. This is because of low self-esteem, the person imagines that another person is against them and responds to lashing back at their imagined victim.

This is one aspect of life where assumptions can lead to major challenges in life. The one who is angry has interpreted that the actions or words of another person is slight and an attack on them.

Rather than raising the pertinent issue with the offending person so as to iron out the issue, they use their interpretation by assuming that any offense, perceived or real, was intentional.

People will not have time and space for you if you are often complaining or angry.

Constructive Anger

Constructively angered people direct their angry emotions in a more positive, constructive way so as to achieve a desirable outcome. You must remember that anger is not often a bad emotion. Anger exists for a positive purpose.

Management Strategy

This is a powerful motivator. Apply it to get over the fear, deal with injustices, and accomplish your desired outcomes in life.

Deliberate Anger

This type of anger is also called motivational anger. Deliberate anger is usually applied by managers, both in sports and at the workplace. The aspect is that when your team sees how angry you are; they will be motivated to enhance their score or performance.

It is usually used as a tool to control fellow workmates, and it does not often last for a long time. The major problem with a ruling by fear is that you have to keep pulling this stunt. Ultimately, your fellow workmates will start to see through it and fail to act, unless you escalate matters.

Behavioral Anger

Oftentimes, those who face this type of anger confront the things that get them angry. And it is often other people. It does not matter whether the other person is sincerely doing something wrong or; the person who is angry is just in a bad mood and interpreting everything in the most negative manner imaginable.

This is a key in understanding when handling anger; it's not the other person's behavior that is getting you angry; it is your response to their behavior that is leading to your angry emotions. These confrontations start with verbal rudeness and usually escalates into physical violence.

For every minute you remain angry, you give up sixty seconds of peace of mind.

Management Strategy

The greatest remedy for anger is a delay. When you feel your anger is rising fast, take a moment, and calm down before you respond. Excuse yourself from the event, if possible, and apply a self-talk tactic to regain control of your feeling until you feel physically calm down. Then you can reconsider what is occurring when you are feeling less agitated.

Chapter 4

Causes of Anger

Emotions of anger arise because of how you interpret and respond to specific events. Every person has the factors that get them angry. These include situations in which you feel:

- Like you are being treated invalidated or unfairly

- Like people are disrespecting your feelings or possessions

- Powerless or frustrated

- Attacked or threatened

- Injustice

- Physical threats

- Relationship issues

- Lack of control

- Abusive language

- Misinformation

People can comprehend particular events differently, so an event that gets you angry may not get another person angry. But because you can comprehend things differently, it does not mean that you are comprehending things wrong when you become angry.

How a person reacts and interprets to an event can rely on many factors in their life, including:

- Past Experiences

  If you have ever experienced events that triggered your angry emotions, such as bullying, abuse or trauma, both as an adult or as a child, and you were not able to appropriately express your anger at that particular time, you might still be coping with those angry emotions currently

  You might now find a situation specifically challenging, and likely to get you angry. At times your current emotions of anger may not be about the present event but may also be linked to a past event, which means that the angry emotions that you are facing are at a level that reflects your past event.

Becoming more aware of your experience can help you to find methods of reacting to events in the present in a more less and safer distressed manner.

- Your Upbringing

How you can cope with angry emotions is usually impacted by your childhood upbringing. Most people are presented with information about angry emotions as a child that may make it difficult to handle it as an adult. For example:

- You may have witnessed your other adult sibling's or parent's anger when it is out of hand and began to think of anger as something terrifying and destructive.

- You may have grown up thinking that it is often right to respond to your anger violently or aggressively. Hence you did not learn how to manage and understand your angry emotions. Meaning that you have angry outburst whenever you don't like the manner in which another person is acting themselves, or whenever you are in the event that you do not like.

- Present Circumstances

When you are encountering many challenges in life, you find yourself getting angry easily than often, or becoming angry at unrelated issues.

If there is a specific thing that is getting you angry, and yet you do not feel able to express your angry emotions directly, then you might find yourself expressing those angry emotions at a later date.

Angry emotions can also be a part of grief. If you have lost a person that you love and care, this event can be largely challenging to handle and manage with all the conflicting issues you might be feeling.

When Is Anger a Problem?

Speak out when you are feeling overwhelmed by angry emotions, and you will make the perfect speech you will ever regret making.

There's certainly no other problematic natural human emotion than anger. You will hear contradictory and endless advice on how to control and manage anger. Examples of such advice:

- "Do not hold anger inside—express it, and let it out."

- "Anger is very bad for your health—so don't easily get angry because you will have a heart attack.

What is to be done? In case that you express out your angry emotions, hold angry emotions inside, and ignore that anger does not exist. None is a healthy alternative.

The issue with angry emotions is not its existence, but how you control and manage your anger. There's no doubt that chronic anger explosions—and angry outburst of arguments are not good for your health. Rage puts you into the flight or fight response where adrenaline is being triggered, and you are on full red alert. When this series of events constantly occurs in your body system, the full alert reaction causes clogged arteries, high blood pressure, and risk of having a heart attack or a stroke.

Most of you were brought up to believe one or more of the following:

- Explosive angry emotions are a sign of power and strength.

- A good guardian never gets angry at their children.

- "If you loved more you would never get angry at me."

- Happily, married spouse never get angry at each other.

- Wives and husbands should never go to bed while they are angry at each other.

- Any person who gets angry is bad.

- Anger is a sign of weakness.

- The only way to express anger is by violence and loud yelling.

- You have no right to get angry at other people.

- You are not accepted when you are at an angry state, and you know that it will lead to rejection.

- Expressing anger is mean and harmful to other people.

The above statements fall under myths of anger, and they are not helpful to you since they describe angry emotions in the most adverse means possible. The truth is that angry emotions can be so useful if applied appropriately and in the appropriate context. Angry emotions should not be applied as a manner to annihilate or control others. It is not a sign of power or strength, particularly when it is aggressive. Applied sparingly and in the perfect manner, angry emotions can clear the air and bring people together.

A challenge that most people face with angry emotions is that they instantly get aggressive. Whether they experience an explosive anger disorder, when they are out of control, they are not assisting anyone or themselves. Part of the issue for these people is to give themselves more time to leave the situation so that they can calm down and relax.

Contrary to the stereotype thinking that angry emotions mean throwing things away and yelling loudly, healthy expression of angry emotions needs you verbally but firmly express your frustration in a controlled way.

Most couples often spend most of their time interrupting and yelling at each other instead of listening. The outcome is a maximizing crescendo of negative feelings that threaten to burst into physical violence. That is why it is advisable to married partners to often engage in a range of physical exercises and practices that teach them how to take turns while speaking, paraphrasing and listening why has been said by the other partner.

When you try to push away and deny a person's anger can cause a feeling of depression and hopelessness. This has occurred many times in the aspect of psychotherapy. Most patients have a challenge in expressing their angry emotions and frustrations with their therapist. This issue reflects the challenges that the patients have with other people in the universe.

In learning how to control and manage one's angry emotions, there are some factors that you should take into consideration prior to expressing those emotions:

- Can you effectively express what is on your mind in a manner that is assertive firm and respectful of both your boundaries and the boundaries of the other person?

- If you express your angry emotions, how will other people react? Will the other people feel hurt, or will they fight back? Could it cause damage to the relationship?

- What is the perfect manner for you to express your frustrations? Yelling is bad for me and anyone else. You know you require to talk about it but in a manner that is assertive and calm

- How vital is it for you to express your angry emotions? If it's a minor issue, the best thing to do letting go.

Effects of Anger

Most people do not view anger as a major problem. When upsetting events occur, maybe breaking of relationship, you are able to deal with the situation without blowing up your emotions.

When you neglect your anger, no one will get to know of your struggle. Outwardly, you seem okay. Inside, you might feel disrespected, and you might feel like your emotions do not count or feel neglected. You do not speak up because you do not want to rock the boat.

Effects of Anger on Your Health

An unhealthy outburst of angry emotions, when you hold angry emotions inside for a long time, it can explode in rage and can cause havoc on your health. If you are prone to losing your temper, the following are vital reasons why you should stay calm:

- Anger triggers a stroke.

Beware, if you are prone to anger outbursts. There are three times higher chances of getting a stroke from a blood clot to the brain or bleeding in the brain during the two hours after an explosive argument. Those with an aneurysm in one of their arteries in the brain, there are six times higher chances of rapturing this aneurysm after an angry argument.

Good news is that one can learn and understand how to manage those angry arguments. For one to move into positive thinking, you require to recognize what your triggers are and then find out how to alter your reaction. Instead of exploding with anger, one can practice deep breathing therapy. Apply assertive communication techniques. One might even require to change their environment.

- Anger can make your anxiety worse.

  If you are a person who gets worried, it is vital to note that anger and anxiety go together—a state characterized by uncontrollable and excessive worry that disrupts a person's daily routine.

- The angry argument puts your heart at significant risk.

Physically injury is anger's impact on your cardiac health. During the two hours after an angry explosion, the chances of cardiac arrest doubles. Repressed anger is related to cardiac arrest. Those with prone to anger as a personality trait are at a double chance of coronary disease than their less angry friends.

To defend yourself, recognize and manage your emotions before you lose your temper any time. Constructive anger, this is the form where you openly talk to the person you are angry with and try to manage the angry emotions in a problem-solving way. This is not linked to heart illness. Constructive anger is a very healthy and natural emotion.

- Anger weakens the immune system.

If you are the kind of person who is always angry, you might find yourself feeling sick always. Healthy people, recall an angry outburst from their past experience, this will lead to a six-hour dip in the levels of antibody immunoglobulin A, the cells' first line of defense against infections.

If you are habitually upset, defend your immune system by learning several effective coping techniques. Using humor, assertive communication, restructuring your thoughts or effective problem solving to escape from the white and black, all or nothing thinking. These are perfect tactics that you can cope with.

- Hostility can harm your lungs.

Not only smokers are a risk of harming their lungs. You still could be harming your lungs if you are often upset. Men with high hostility ratings have a worse lung capacity that maximizes their chances of respiratory disorders. An uptake in stress hormones that are related to angry emotions builds inflammation in the air vents in the lungs.

- Anger is related to depression.

Depression is linked with angry explosion and aggression, specifically in men. In the aspect of passive anger, depression where you ruminate about depression, but you never act, is very popular. A piece of advice to deal with this effect is to get very busy and stop thinking a lot.

A physical activity that absorbs you is a perfect cure for angry emotions, such as cycling and golf. These activities tend to fill your mind fully and pull your concentration toward the current situation, and there is just no room left for angry emotions to crop up when you have got that activity going on.

How Unexpressed Anger Influences Communication

If you are upset, it stimulates a freeze, fight or flight response that impacts the capability to hear what is being said. Many outbursts escalate not because of what is said but what you think is being said.

Passive anger, this is where anger is not actively expressed. It is denied an outlet; hence, it leaks out in means you do not expect, such as saying okay when you mean you're not okay.

Most people assume that by neglecting angry emotions, they can avoid potential issues. Those who do not like feuds avoid confrontations, but finally, the unexpressed angry emotion piles up in the form of resentment. Stress becomes a major problem because you are attempting to shove the emotions away.

How You Can Tackle This
If you are sharing your emotional issues with a close friend, keep the concentration on yourself and how you feel when you get angry. Avoid utterances that criticize or blame other people for your responses. Acknowledging your facts avoid blame and invite cooperation.

How Unchecked Anger Impacts Your Emotions
You cannot deal with your emotions without identifying the emotions that you experience first. For example, fear is usually felt in the stomach; anger manifests in the head and the upper part of the body. Happiness radiates from the center and is felt all over the body. Sadness feels like a heavy heart.

After you have identified how you feel emotionally, it is vital not to judge yourself for possessing those emotions. Emotions are not bad or good. Emotions are a natural aspect of your life. Identifying those emotions takes practice and a willingness to be more gentle with self.

How You Can Tackle This
Usually, avoiding feelings cause addictive habits like using drugs and alcohol, specifically when upset. Any compulsive practice acts to cover up the pain. So instead, you should permit for you to feel all the emotions and remember to be mindful about your emotions. Name the emotions and pick healthier means to process the emotions.

How Unchecked Anger Impacts Your Values
Naturally, you do not have any urge to hurt a person. But if angry emotions are suppressed for a long period, anger gets very hard to manage. Even the most mild-mannered individual can face anger outburst because denied anger has to leak out ultimately. The more that angry emotions are denied, the more the emotions may

cause abusive habits, even if that is not your norm. That is why identifying the emotion at an early time is so vital.

How You Can Tackle This

Always pay close attention when you require a time out. Always identify and understand early warning signs of angry emotion so as to assess when to remove yourself from the event. Understanding when to leave an anger argument keeps every person safe.

Effects of Anger on Trust

If you do not honor anger, then a false image gets created. You say everything is okay, but you do not seem okay. People-pleasing habits become a means to avoid a clash and gain approval. This is usually the start of codependency. Pretending to be something that you are not creating more problematic issues.

Friends and family will not understand what to expect since your demeanor and tone do not match. When angry emotion is denied outlet, it creates confusion in a relationship since others have no idea what is disturbing you. You may feel invisible and secretly resentful.

How You Can Tackle This

You should know that a healthy relationship succeeds in authenticity. Accepting what is disturbing you takes a lot of courage, but it also rebuilds a broken trust. Those who love and care about you do want to hear and understand what you have to say to them.

Motivational Effects of Anger

It gives a mixture of motivational advantages, some healthy and some self-destructive and some short-sighted effects.

On the positive aspect, anger builds a feeling of control and power in an event where prior to anger these motivating, positive emotions were not there. The feelings of righteousness and control that emanate from anger can motivate you to change and challenge hard social injustices and interpersonal injustices. When you handle anger appropriately, it can motivate other people to assist you in achieving your desire.

Anger can provide you with a rest from feeling vulnerable, and a means to air out your frustrations and tensions. Anger provides the resolve and energy essential to protect yourself when you have been attacked.

If you have been suffering from domestic abuse, and your angry emotions reach the optimal level, it will enable you to part ways with your abusive relationship or partner. Anger has truly been a positive force in your life.

If you are dedicated crusader to further a moral purpose, then anger gives you the necessary strength to carry on, and the will power to persevere.

Meanwhile, it creates and reinforces a false feeling of entitlement, an illusory sense of moral superiority that can be applied to justify sinful reactions. For example, anger motivates aggression that can be applied to justify terrorism or bully another person into performing what you desire them to perform against their own will.

People who are angry are prone to subscribe to the philosophy that the end justifies the meaning and then apply unspeakable ways of working towards their achievements that defeat their aim.

Accepting Your Anger

One of the significant steps in managing your anger is by admitting that you are angry. Recognizing the emotional feelings of anger, understanding why and how to deal with them is essential in managing and controlling anger. Denial of your feelings can cause severe emotional and physical damage to an individual. The first thing to do is to sort out and identify your emotional feelings; this helps you in accepting other people's beliefs altogether.

Causes of Anger

When anger is left to internalize in an individual, it can be an emotional time bomb that can explode anytime when easily triggered by little issues. Anger may be triggered by feelings of not being appreciated, overexploited, being manipulated, feeling humiliated, being a failure, and feeling neglected. As a woman, you can learn to control your emotions by understanding the different types of feelings and the kind of anger they can cause.

Coping with Anger

Most of the time, anger is triggered by blame. When you blame yourself or other people, it is a way of running away from the actual problem that you are facing. Energy and time spent by the individual blaming other people can be used better by working on ways to understand your feelings.

Reaction to Anger

Was your response justified? Did your reaction to anger increase the level of stress in your body or risk the relationship you had with the people around you? If the answer is yes, you should find a better way to release your anger without hurting people around you who care about you and love you. It is healthy and confident to talk to other people about your feelings and share with them your situation. Talking to people more realistically and also using relaxation techniques to air out your opinions is a sure way to deal with anger.

Is your Anger reasonable? You should often ask yourself this question before you react to anger. Do not expect too much from yourself or other people because this will not raise your expectations.

Understanding Your Feelings

When you are not in a position of identifying and thinking about your feelings when angry, it may be so stressful for you. Having feelings is a natural thing, but recognizing that they exist and accepting them is more important to your mental health.

Ways of Accepting Your Feelings

Sharing with Others

You should not keep your feelings private for a long time. Sharing your experience with people around you who care about you or people who are in a similar situation can make them lend a helping hand or necessary support. By doing this, you will find out that you are not the only person facing the problem.

Sharing It with Your Family Members

Family members are the people who are close to you. Most of the times, another member of your family may have gone through the same feeling before, sharing with such a person may help you find a solution quickly. Besides, it enables you to express, and it constructively accepts your beliefs and feelings. Being together as a family can also help provide reassurance and support to one another and assist in building each other's self-esteem.

Time Management

Try to make the most out of your time. Avoid sleeping late and spending much of your time watching television. Spend most of your time with your kids and husband, work on your projects, and also visit friends. Good time management skills will make you feel more productive and may provide you with a job opportunity if you are unemployed.

It is essential for you to accept and own your feelings of anger, thus assisting you in a big way to understand other people's feelings in the end, thus helping you control your emotions. If rage is left to internalize in a person, it will have adverse effects on the individual that may later be regretful; hence, the need to accept and own our feelings of anger.

Challenging Your Anger

Anger is a feeling that is natural, and everyone has different ways of expressing their outrage. It is a natural response to attack or threaten a person's life. It is a powerful emotion that makes it difficult in releasing the pressure that is generated inside someone making it almost impossible to deal with problems and move on.

In this chapter, we will talk about how anger works and learn the benefits of controlling your anger at a level that is not harmful to your body and the people close to you. Also, we will get to understand the various ways you can use to challenge your anger more effectively and economically.

How Anger Works

During our daily routine, we always have thoughts about different situations and decide about them: safe or not safe, bad or good. We interpret these situations, considering how we feel about each happening. If a circumstance is right, we feel safe, and if it is terrible, we feel threatened or afraid. If someone has wronged you, you may feel angry. The feeling determines how we will react to the situation. At times the speed at which we respond to anger makes us regret in the future.

When you are being brought up during childhood, you observe many situations and events and associate them. From these experiences, children learn to handle every circumstance as they learned and saw when they were growing up.

Managing Your Anger

Here are some practical means to calming down:

Buying Time

When you first feel the urge to be angry, pause for some time, and think about what has made you angry, think of the resulting consequences of you reacting with anger. Making that pause for a moment delays your reaction and can make a big difference in coming up with a wiser decision than just acting immediately. It will also help you deal with the situation more constructively. Additionally, it can be applied during arguments by taking a deep breath and choosing how you will express your feelings positively.

Rational Thinking

Drop off your shoulders then take a deep breath. It helps you to relax, letting your instinct to change the earlier decision of getting your body ready to fight to rational self that reserves the message by allowing your body to chill out. Always make sure you count from ten to one before acting.

If you are in a situation in which you feel the urge of throwing something or hitting out at something hit something soft like a cushion that you cannot damage or hurt. Expressing yourself in writing rather than facing the person also helps. Talking yourself down has also been proven to be the best way of easing your anger.

Talking to a friend who may help you get a different view or perspective on the situation might be very helpful. Besides, you can try having an image of yourself in a relaxing scene. Distracting yourself by reading a magazine or listening to smooth music helps you forget the terrible experience. You should work off your anger through physical exercise. This helps channel your energy to other activities that make your brain feels better and relaxed. Use of other relaxing techniques such a meditation or Yoga can also help a great deal in easing anger.

Being Assertive

Being assertive is for people who find it difficult to speak up. It is a healthier way of expressing anger than aggression. When you are in a situation of bursting up with anger, you allow yourself to take another gear and take control of your feelings. You can control your anger by trying the following activities:

- Talking clearly and slowly

- Using the word "I" to make it your own

- Requesting rather than demanding

- Talking to people and telling them you are feeling angry and the reasons why

Knowing Yourself

It can be beneficial for you to understand and know what makes you angry and how it makes you behave. Try it out when you are sober and in a good mood. Being a good problem solver can help you avoid feeling like a victim when things do not go well. You should know and understand that some problems are beyond your control.

Mental Health Protection

Being stressed out makes you feel like losing temper. Therefore, it is appropriate for you to maintain good mental health since it helps you cope when things go in the wrong direction. It is advisable that you try doing the following actions to ensure you protect your mental health:

- Being caring for others

- Accepting who you are and concentrate on the things you can do correctly

- Having time to relax and enjoy yourself

- Being physically active

- Having a balanced diet

- Taking certain types of food that are more effective in supplying a steady flow of energy to the body, which then aids in the proper functioning

- Regular bursting and checking out on friends who you may talk to about your feelings, as well as asking for assistance whenever necessary

Chapter 5

Understanding Your Mental Health and Anger

Mental Health

This refers to your cognitive, behavioral, and emotional well-being—it is about how you feel, behave, and think.

Mental health is a condition of well-being that a person understands their capabilities, can manage the natural stress of life, can perform fruitfully and productively, and can contribute to the well-being of the society.

It is also defined as the absence of behavioral or mental illness—a condition of psychological well-being that a person has accomplished a satisfactory integration of a person's natural, instinctual urge acceptable to both one's social milieu and oneself.

Mental Disorder

It means a variety of mental conditions—these are disorders that influence your behavior, thinking, and mood. Such as addictive behaviors, schizophrenia, eating disorders, depression, and anxiety disorders.

Symptoms

Symptoms and signs of mental disorder can vary, relying on the illness, circumstances, and several factors. Mental disorder symptoms can impact behaviors, emotions, and thoughts.

Symptoms and signs of having a mental disorder include:

- Sex urge changes

- Suicidal thinking

- Major changes in eating behaviors

- Excessive violence, upset, and hostility

- Problems with drug abuse and alcohol

- Lack of ability to cope with your daily stress

- Having trouble relating and understanding of events and people

- Withdrawal from activities and friends

- Hallucinations, delusions, and paranoia

- Excessive fears or worries

- Extreme mood changes

- Feeling down or sad

- Reduced ability to concentrate or confused thinking

Sometimes, symptoms of mental illness manifest as physical problems, for example, headaches, stomach or back pain.

When to Visit a Doctor

If you show any symptoms or signs of a mental disorder, visit your Primary care provider. Many mental illnesses do not enhance on their own, and if not treated urgently, a mental illness may get worse and even cause serious medical issues.

When Having Suicidal Thinking

Suicidal behavior and thoughts are popular with various mental disorders. When you think of hurting yourself or commit suicide, you should get assistance urgently:

- Contact your mental health specialist.

- Call a spiritual minister or a person in your faith community.

- Seek immediate assistance from your health provider.

- Call a suicide hotline number. Call the National Prevention Lifeline at 1-800-273-TALK (1-800-273-8255).

Assist a Person You Love

When the person you care about and love manifests signs of mental illness, have an honest and open interaction with him/her about your concerns. You might not be able to force the person to get professional care, but you can offer support and encouragement.

Causes of Mental Problems or Illnesses

Environment

Being exposed to environmental toxins, drugs, alcohol, stressors, or inflammatory conditions can, at times, be related to mental illness.

Brain Chemistry

Neurotransmitters are normally occurring brain chemicals that provide signals to other parts of your body and brain. If the neural networks consisting of these chemicals are destroyed, the function of the nerve system and nerve receptors change, causing depression and other emotional disorders.

Inherited Traits

Mental disorder is more popular in people whose blood relatives have a mental illness. Particular genes may maximize your likelihood of developing a mental illness, and your life situation may stimulate it.

Risk Factors

Particular triggers may maximize your risk of developing a mental disorder, including:

- Traumatic brain injury as an outcome of serious brain damage

- An ongoing chronic medical condition such as diabetes

- Previous mental disorder

- Childhood history of neglect or abuse

- Few healthy relationships or few friends

- Use of recreational drugs or alcohol

- Traumatic experiences

- Stressful situations, such as the death of a person you love, financial problems, or divorce

- Having a history of mental disorder in a first-degree relative

Mental disorder can start at any given age, from childhood to adult life, but most instances start early in life. The impacts of mental disorder can be long-lasting or temporary. A person can have multiple mental disorder at the same time.

Complications

Mental illness is a leading contributing factor to disability. A mental disorder that is left untreated can lead to severe physical health, behavioral, and emotional problems. Complications sometimes are linked to the mental disorder include:

- Heart disease

- Having a weak immune system, hence your body has difficulty in resisting infections

- Homelessness and poverty

- Harm to others and self-harm including homicide and suicide

- Financial and legal problems

- Social isolation

- Decreased enjoyment in life and unhappiness

- Relationship difficulties

- Family conflicts.

Prevention

There are no specific means to prevent mental disorders. However, when you suffer from a mental disorder, you need to take steps to manage stress and anger in your life, you need to understand and learn how to manage your anger emotions. This will enhance your resilience and boost your low self-esteem may assist in keeping your symptoms under control.

Steps to follow:

- Pay close attention to warning signs.

  Engage your therapist to learn and understand what might trigger your symptoms. Create a plan so that you understand what to do if symptoms appear again. Often contact your therapists if you realize any change in your symptoms or how you are feeling. Make some consideration of involving your family to be watchful for early warning signs.

- Routine Medical Care

  Avoid ignoring appointments with your health clinic, particularly if you are not feeling okay. You may be experiencing a new health issue that requires to be checked and treated urgently, or you may be experiencing side effects of the medication.

- Get assistance when you need it.

  Mental disorder can be difficult to treat if you sit and wait until symptoms get worse. Long term management treatment also may assist in preventing a relapse of signs and symptoms.

- Take good care of yourself.

Enough sleep, regular physical exercise, and healthy eating are very key. Maintain a regular routine that you follow. Have talks with your primary care provider if you have problems in sleeping or matters about physical exercise and your diet.

Common Mental Illness or Disorders

The most popular forms of mental disorder are schizophrenia, anxiety, and mood disorders.

Below they are explained in detail:

Mood Disorders

Also referred to as depressive or affective disorder. People with this condition have severe alterations in mood, primarily consists of either depression or elation.

Examples include:

1. Major depression – A person is no longer enjoys or like events and activities that they enjoyed or liked previously. There are serious periods of sadness.

2. Seasonal affective disorder (SAD) – This is a major kind of depression that is stimulated by inadequate daylight. SAD is popular in countries far from the equator during the season of late autumn, early spring, and winter.

3. Bipolar disorder – The person shifts from a series of euphoria despair. This is previously called manic-depressive illness.

4. Persistent depressive disorder – This is mild despair. The person has the same symptoms to major depression but a lesser extent.

Schizophrenia Disorders

It is a single disorder that has yet to be completely established. Schizophrenia is a very complex disorder. It usually starts between the age of fifteen to twenty-five. The person has many episodes of thought processes that appear fragmented; finding it difficult to process the information.

It has positive and negative symptoms and signs. Positive symptoms consist of hallucinations, delusions, and thought disorders. Negative symptoms consist of inappropriate mood, withdrawal, or inadequate motivation.

Anxiety Disorders
This is the most popular form of mental disorder. The patient has extreme anxiety or fear, that is related to particular situations or objects. Many people with this illness will attempt to avoid whatever exposure to what stimulates their anxiety levels.

Anxiety disorders include:

1. Post-traumatic stress disorder (PSTD) – PSTD happens after someone has experienced a traumatic situation—something frightening or horrible that they have witnessed or experienced. During this situation, the person thinks that his/her life is in total danger. The patient may feel extremely afraid, and the person has no control over what is occurring.

2. Phobias – These consist of simple quite phobias such as social phobias; fear of being a victim to

the judgment of other people, and agoraphobia; fearful of events where escaping or breaking away may be hard.

Treatment

There are different means people suffering from mental disorder might get treatment. It's vital to understand that a treatment that works for one person may not be effective for another person.

- Medication – Although it may not effectively cure mental illness, some medications can enhance symptoms

- Self-help – It involves lifestyle alterations, for example, reducing alcohol intake, eat well, and sleeping sufficiently.

- Psychotherapy – This is a psychological method of treating mental disorder. Dialectical behavior therapy, cognitive behavioral therapy, and exposure therapy are examples of therapies.

Understanding Your Anger

Anger is a normal emotion designed in a flight-or-fight response by the physiology of your body and mind. If you feel a slight threat, your mind produces anger and fear. The fear produced is part of the flight reaction from your physiology.

Anger is the emotional energy that you produce for the fight against that perceived danger. What is confusing is that your mind generates anger and fear, even when the danger is imagined.

Emotions, such as anger, are real and natural. Even if the danger is imagined, the anger that you generate is as powerful and practical. However, the purposes you produce anger are not often actual. When you are not aware of how your mind is imagining events of hurt, your anger will manifest irrational.

Imagined vs. Real Anger

Sometimes, it is hard to distinguish an actual danger from imagined danger, as they occur at a specific time. For instance, when someone is cutting you off on the highway, and a car briefly maneuvers in a manner that could lead to an accident and possibly harm you. There is a natural flight or fight response to your emotion, and you generate a combination of anger and fear. The reality of this threat often passes fast, and so do your feelings.

However, your imaginations may take over and generate worse instances. You start considering that you or another person in your vehicle might be killed or hurt. You may call the same situation from your experience, and project those instances into your mind and add more feelings. After the physical danger goes through your brain, your mind still projects instances in the imagination. Your emotion then reacts to those imaginations.

The emotions that you generate from your imaginations are no longer tied on anything actual. Because of the natural reactions of your emotions to what you imagine, you are able to amplify anger and fear to the level that they get out of control. However, the anger and fear are natural outcomes of the imaginations. The issue is that imaginations in the brain are out of control and no longer tied in reality.

Awareness

Being not aware of how your imagined instances are projecting these scenarios, you will blame others unnecessarily for your feelings. Proper understanding of how your mind dreams of images and instances of outcome is important to understand your emotions.

Anger Is Rational

It is a normal emotional reaction created to defend you from harm or threat. Anger is part of your instincts from preservation and protection. A mother bear will go into ferocious anger if you try to go near her cubs. It is a force of emotional energy that you safeguard for you to fend off danger.

However, it stops to be a type of protection and becomes a way of destroying your life and relationship when the danger is not actual.

Your emotions react similarly to whether a threat is part of your imagination or real. Anger by itself is a fully rational emotion to possess when you perceive the thoughts and instances in your brain. There's no aspect that is irrational with anger from imagined beliefs and instances. Your natural emotional reaction system is functioning properly. The big issue is with your beliefs, scenarios, and thought in your brain that produces an anger reaction.

You may desire to stop your angry emotions, but it is just a response to another thing. Anger is an emotional response to what your brain and imagination are performing. The means to get over anger is to change how the brain imagines and how much you believe the imaginations. If your mind imagines painful imaginations, you will naturally generate angry emotions. In order to eliminate and reduce angry emotions, it is essential to shift what your brain imagines.

In order to effectively eliminate or reduce angry emotions in your life, alter your core beliefs, interpretation, and assumptions of your brain.

The Reaction to Emotional Pain

Your brain can produce fear and angry emotions, even when there is no physical harm to pain. Your natural emotional reaction system can produce angry emotions just by imagining an instance involving the harm of emotional pain. If your brain is out of control imagining instances of emotional pain, then your anger goes out of control. For angry emotions to occur the emotional pain does not have to happen. When you imagine that you will be hurt in the future, you can get angry before anything has occurred.

Reasons for Understanding Your Anger

Anger can be an incredibly destructive emotion. It is an emotion that is vital for you to understand very well. Here are ideas for understanding your anger:

1. Anger is frequently experienced. Anger is faced much more than any other emotion that many people would want to accept. When you disdain

other people, or when you are frustrated, irritated, or annoyed, you are likely to face some anger. The outcome of research suggests that many couples face the emotion of rage a minimum of eight to ten times a day, and that is prior to having kids.

2. Anger is a secondary feeling. Anger is often experienced in reaction to a primary feeling such as fear, frustration, and harm. It is almost an automatic reaction to any form of pain. Anger is an emotion that most of you experience just after you have been hurt. If your partner corrects you in public, that hurts, and you may react to them in anger. At that particular time, it may be the one emotion that you know and understand, yet it is rarely the one that you have faced.

3. Anger is a fact of life. An important aspect of being human is that you were created in God's image. Part of what it means to be made in

God's image is that you, like God, have a range of feelings and are able to face the feelings of other people. One of these feelings is anger. Anger is a strong feeling of displeasure or irritation. When you face anger, your brain and your body prepare you to respond. Anger consists of emotional and physical energy. It is you to decide whether to apply that energy in constructive means or to abuse yourself and those that you love.

4. Anger is one of the most powerful natural emotions. It provides great energy to right wrongs and alters things for the better. But when you let anger to control you, it can lead to negative, destructive reactions, such as emotional, physical, or verbal abuse. In any romantic relationship, there will be occasions where you will be wronged and hurt. If this occurs, anger can distort your perspective, block your capability to love and hence limit your capability to view things more clearly.

5. Healthy anger has great potential for good. Many people consider angry emotion as something negative, a severe problem, something that requires to be solved and gotten rid of. What you usually fail to view is that every single problem is actually an opportunity in disguise, and opportunity to mature, to learn, to grow, to be applied make greater changes for the better.

6. Anger is a signal. This is a natural feeling that God can apply to get your attention and focus and to make you more aware of opportunities to learn, to mature, to grow, to deepen and to create greater changes for the better. Anger, like love, is a natural emotion that has a greater potential for both evil and good. That is why anger is very vital for you to learn and understand it better

7. Unhealthy anger has greater potential to hurt. At one point in your life, you have been pushed

so hard and get so angry that you could have, or indeed have, get very destructive.

Recently I came across some statistics that clearly show the potential threat of angry emotions that is out of control:

- More than seventy percent of murderers do not have a criminal record.

- Sixty percent of all homicide was committed by persons who knew the victim very well.

- Twenty-seven percent of all police officers killed are murdered while breaking up domestic arguments.

- Ten million kids were beaten by angry guardians, two-thirds of the kids under the age of three.

What Does Keep an Anger Problem Going?

There can be a noticeable pattern to what occurs prior and after an angry outburst. For instance, whilst driving, looking after the kids, or whatever you are talking about. It might be that you are getting into a habit of becoming angry in such contexts. This might be hard to break away from.

There may be consequences of your angry emotions habit—both benefits and cost. Most people recognize that angry behavior can achieve short term gain. For instance, getting your way or having others respect your status. It can also be related to greater long term costs such as damaged long term relationship. Considering these for yourself, it might encourage a change or convince you that you require to take action.

When viewing more closely at the factors that prevent you from getting over anger issues, it gets clear that your behavior, physical sensation, emotions, and thoughts all interact and couple to keep your problems with anger persisting.

Chapter 6

How to Manage Your Anger

Proper Anger Management Is Anger Prevention

At this point, you probably wouldn't need to be explained how destructive angry emotions can be. You are already motivated to bring desired changes in your emotionally controlled habits. Emotional patterns require just more than intellectual knowledge from reading to practical changes. In this chapter, you will be assisted to understand much better what you are handling and a process that is not just to control and manage but to fully get rid of your angry emotions responses.

A Different Method to Anger Management

Anger is a very destructive emotional force, just like fire. Anger can cause damage to your relationship, business, career, and home. I would not try to control a fire in my house or relationship. No matter the size of the fire, it can perform extreme harm. This is why the appropriate means of managing fire is preventing the fire from occurring. On the same context, the perfect form of managing your angry emotions is anger prevention.

Traditional anger therapy is channeled on ways to manage your behaviors and emotions immediately. Thereafter, you will learn how to recognize triggers that ignite you into angry emotions so that you can remain ahead of anger. This does not mean that you have resolved your angry emotions problem. It means that you have learned and understood compensating techniques to avoid anger and distract yourself prior to the actual negative reaction.

In the aspect of prevention of angry emotions, you go after the underlying cause that ignites your angry emotions. Not only learning to recognize the catalyst of your angry emotions but dissolving and eliminating the patterns in the brain triggering those catalysts. The emotional forces that control the patterns of angry emotions are beliefs, particularly beliefs that are not true; you then use several practical activities that will make you fade away the emotions. If you alter those untrue beliefs, you no longer need to control and manage your angry emotion. You do not have to avoid or manage your anger because it no longer exists.

The Key to Anger Prevention

This is the identification of false beliefs as the root cause of your angry emotions. Beliefs are the elemental structure of your brain that makes you produce particular thoughts and interpretation about certain things. Beliefs that ate not true, combined with other elements such as point of view, coupled to generate a negative emotional response. Two main ingredients to your angry emotions are a perception of being abused and fear. False beliefs are a part of the two ingredients. Usually, mental instances controlling the abuse and fears are not true. Instances can also occur in the brain below a person's point of self-awareness.

Anger is a flight or fights survival reaction to true abuse or harm. Your emotions react similarly to the instances that you imagine. When fear or abuse is in the imagined instance, angry emotions will still be the emotional response, but the leading factors cannot be seen. This makes anger seem irrational.

Your brain can produce emotional abuse and fear via instances that you imagine. You can refer to instances as projections of untrue beliefs. Imagining a person abusing you in a particular manner can have a similar impact on your emotions as if it were occurring. Adopting a different point of view about imaginations is a big factor that can alter this dynamic. Altering your point of view is an aspect that you can learn and understand how to perform it in the Self Mastery Audio Program via several practical activities.

Altering your false belief and point of view needs a bit of more introspective work than just taking deep breaths or counting to ten. It consists of learning techniques to pay close attention to the brain and dissect some of the beliefs that are hidden in the brain. In this method, you will also learn what not to perform, so that you don't make yourself feel bad about what you find out. After that, you will use some techniques to alter the dynamics going on in your brain that are at the root cause of your upset. The outcome of these techniques can result in permanent change.

Inventory of Beliefs

The process of changing and identifying the core beliefs that are the underlying cause of your angry emotion is the self-mastery audio practice. There are various techniques that you will understand in practicing the activities in the program. Apart from understanding how to alter the point of view, you will also be taking a core belief inventory. For you to achieve this process, it is not essential to take an inventory of every principle in your life. You can write an inventory of particular emotional responses and issues that you experience.

Writing an inventory of core beliefs is like solving a mystery of what is occurring inside your brain. The mystery is all about determining the core beliefs that drive your angry emotions. Most people think of this process as learning your triggers. No, it's not. By writing an inventory, you explore and observe the unconscious part of the brain that is positioned below the catalyst.

Core Belief Inventory: Anger

The process of developing self-mastery needs that you be fully honest with yourself. One of the tactics to help in this full honesty is the core belief inventory. By making an inventory, you can break away from the layers of false beliefs, denial, projection, image, and ego. In this manner, you have the chance to be very authentic.

Most people think that you will unravel your beliefs by writing down the thoughts in your mind—when you do that you will be missing most of the underlying beliefs below those thoughts. There are more effective means.

Self-Awareness

Self-awareness is the capability to have a clear perception of your personality make up, including your motivation, core beliefs, emotions, strengths, thoughts, and weaknesses. It let you learn other people, how they perceive you, your responses, and your attitude at that moment.

You can quickly assume that you understand, but it is meaningful to possess a relative scale for awareness. If you have ever experienced an auto-clash, you may have noticed every detail occurring in slow motion and recognized the details of your thought process and the situation. With more practice, you can learn how to engage these forms of extreme conditions and see new alternatives for interpretations in your thoughts, interactions, and emotions. Having self-awareness does create a chance to make a change in beliefs and behavior.

Below are two scenarios of the causes of anger that were discovered via the process of inventory. By engaging in some practices in self-awareness, these two people were able to start to change their behaviors and expressions immediately. However, once their untrue beliefs were discovered, the angry emotions of these two people started to fade away.

Anger Scenario 1: How Self-Abuse Causes Angry Emotions

Mike habitually had angry arguments to his spouse for the little issues. He has been performing this for years and did not know the reason. After each outburst, Mike would make a promise never to do it. Mike could hold back his frustrations for a long time, but ultimately, an argument would burst out. The outcome would be a punishing reply from a voice in his head about how terrible his reaction was and what a miserable human he is.

In a similar event, Mike was driving with his kids and wife. Mike's spouse picked some trash from the console to clean up, and that triggered a fiery explosion from Mike. Mike snapped at the wife and released out a toxic venom. Having the kids in the vehicle Mike got a hold of his venom words, but rather he raged from inside for many more kilometers.

You can think that angry emotion is something that can occur to less unaccomplished or educated people. Mike is an engineer. In spite of the level of education, Mike's training did not consist of changing and identifying his beliefs or the process his brain generated emotions. With all the intelligence, Mike could not make any reason for his explosive outbursts until he started paying close attention to his inner core beliefs and dialog.

Mike began to use self-mastery and self-awareness exercises tactics. Mike applied the process of taking inventory mentioned in the self-mastery practice to investigate and alter the root cause of his angry emotion. By altering his point of view, and maximizing his self-awareness beliefs, emotions, and his thoughts, Mike was able to fade away a large percentage of his angry emotions as well as making changes in another aspect of his life.

Anger Scenario 2: How Fear Can Be a Source of Angry Emotions

Zack worked in various enterprises and had quit each company under similar conditions or frustration and anger. Zack realized he could not afford to keep quitting jobs, and that prompted him to ask for assistance from qualified personnel. This had taken a financial loss in the past, and Zack did not want to continue with the destructive financial and emotional pattern.

Zack thought that he understood the pattern, but Zack did see how to alter the pattern. Zack attempted to will his angry emotions away, but that worked for a short while. Zack's effort at personal development and self-help methods made temporary advancements, but Zack would relapse back to the serious problem of angry emotions. In various practices, Zack's self-help trials made things worse, as Zack would judge himself for failing after a relapse and feel even worse.

Zack primarily understood the emotional process well, to begin with, feeling not appreciated. Zack would attempt so hard to gain approval and recognition, but somehow it did not work. Zack would work very hard for the people around him but still did not feel that he was more appreciated and recognized for the extra work. With time Zack felt upset at the people around him for their lack of appreciation and caring. At a particular time, he would get more frustrated and upset with his work that he would give up.

Through various self-awareness practices, Zack started to recognize some factors that stimulate his emotions, that which he had not discovered. One of the catalysts was the feeling of fear. Zack was very busy trying to make every internal client happy that he did not notice the level of fear was that was behind his motivation. Zack was very afraid of disappointing the internal clients. He was so afraid that the internal clients would judge him. Zack was very afraid of letting the internal clients down. Zack was very afraid that the internal clients would get upset. Most crucial Zack was frightened that he would get punished.

Zack's brain spent most of the time imagining instances where other people would get angry. The people rarely got angry, but that did not stop Zack's imaginations. Zack generation of angry emotions was a natural emotional reaction to feeling mistreated, even if the unfair treatment was imagined. Zack's emotions were a rational reaction.

Zack's fear of being punished was inventoried—he imagined of instances of experience from his childhood of a specific harsh tutor. Zack recalled being frightened of attending the class because of how the teacher mistreated him. Zack was asked to pay close attention to the instances in his imagination spun about the people at work and saw if there were any differences between women and men workmates. Zack did not feel mistreated from any male workmate. Zack's fear instances all involved women.

It was found that a defining element in Zack's experience where the imaginations began to flash instances of fear. Related to that situation was a set of core beliefs about himself getting punished unfairly. This aspect was associated specifically to how women in positions of power mistreated him. Zack's mind continued to imagine assumptions about his future and present events based on the beliefs he learned from the past.

A mistake most people do in attempting to get rid of their angry emotions is to look for one particular thing to change. There are often various components that conspire together in the brain to generate an emotional response. When you look for one simple component, you are likely to miss out on the large element of the problem.

Finding the Root Cause of Anger
Through inventory-taking, Mike was able to identify that the underlying cause of his anger towards the spouse was simple self-judgment. Mike couldn't view all this since he did not know where and how to look at his thoughts from an observer point of view. Mike also did not understand how his thoughts were capable of his emotional response.

Return on Your Investment

Taking your time to perform a core belief inventory and become more aware of the dynamics of the brain that trigger your behavior and emotions is not a quick fix. You can start by making changes in your behavior instantly, but fully fading away, your angry emotions will take a bit longer. However, it is a long term solution, and it can be permanent.

At times you will identify and alter some core beliefs at that particular moment. Other times it will take you up to a few weeks, to develop the techniques to alter your point of view and identity and alter the beliefs and interpretation.

Gaining full control of your emotional responses is like continuing to put out a fire. This is what many anger management methods try to achieve. Anger prevention deals with regaining full control over the core beliefs and interpretation that are at the root cause of your anger and emotions, so you do not have to full control over emotions that you do not need to put out any more fires.

If you have a genuine urge to get rid of unwanted and unnecessary angry emotions from your relationship and life, then you should consider investing more time and effort in yourself. Take more of your time to be aware of your internal beliefs, dialog, and how they impact your angry emotions and how you can alter your emotions. With that awareness, you can alter what passes through your brain and eliminate your angry feelings permanently.

Communication

Clear communication lets you express yourself and get your message across to other people. Engaged and careful listening also assist you in understanding what other people have to say. Good communication techniques can assist you to be better understood. You may also see improvements in your relationships.

Expressing Yourself

- Express your emotions in a perfect and considerable manner. Avoid applying an angry or confrontational approach. Otherwise, this may lead to the other person reacting in frustration, hurt, or fear.

- Often try to be as clear as possible.

- Do not instantly fight back or get defensive. Try to understand more about what the other person feels and what they have said what they said.

- Always think before you say anything. Also, consider what other people might say or think from your comments.

Listening to Others

- Always try to understand the meaning and feelings expressed by others. It can be meaningful to know why they are saying something to you.

- Don't always jump into conclusion or try to mind read your partner. Ask questions if you are not sure.

- Try and avoid misunderstanding and assumption. You could do this by repeating or paraphrasing what has been said. Check whether you have clearly understood.

- Listen attentively to what other people are saying. Do not get distracted.

Styles of Communication

There are a variety of communication styles that different people apply at different times. Some styles are more effective and appropriate than other styles, depending on the situation. The styles include:

Aggressiveness

- You ignore others and do not listen to their views and expressed needs.

- You are often your point through.

- You cannot stand not getting your way done.

- You prioritize your needs above the needs of other people.

This style can be quite confrontational that can cause alienation. Other people may feel that they are not enjoying being around you because they do not take their views into consideration.

Assertiveness

- You have respect for yourself and others.

- You take enough time and listen to the views of other people.

- You believe that every person should have an opportunity to express their needs and opinions.

- You express a preference before discussing in a polite and constructive manner.

- You try to balance your needs against the needs of other people.

Being assertive is all about achieving the perfect balance between two extremes of passive and aggressive communication styles. It can be difficult to be assertive—particularly if you feel intimidated or anxious by an event. It may assist to practice specific strategies and techniques.

Being assertive involves being aware of your needs. You can then express those needs with confidence. Your approach and attitude should be considerate, calm, and confident.

Passiveness

- You can't stand being criticized.

- Find it hard to say No to a person.

- You fear people in power or authority.

- You do not make known your desires or needs.

- You prioritize the needs of others over your own.

- You go along with what others want to be done.

This style means that you do not feel listened to by other people. You might feel that you are a walkover. If such a pattern is created, then people may not expect to hear your views. They can become used to neglecting you. You may end up accepting work or favors despite feeling that they may be unfair.

Chapter 7

Anger Management Techniques

Why Do You Need to Manage Anger?

Anger is a natural feeling that can vary from severe irritation to extreme rage.

While most people consider it as a negative feeling, anger can be very positive. Angry emotions may cause you to stand up for a person or anger can inspire you to create a positive social change.

When anger is left unexpressed angry emotions can cause an aggressive response, such as damaging property or yelling. Angry emotions can make you withdraw from the universe and turn it inward.

Too much frustration can take a toll on you, mentally, physically, and socially. Management techniques are meant to assist you to recognize healthy means to express and reduce your emotions.

You can start by considering the following anger management tips:

Cognitive Behavioral Techniques

Most research shows that cognitive behavioral techniques are more effective techniques for enhancing the management of anger.

It involves changing the manner in which a person behaves and thinks. Cognitive behavioral methods are tied on the understanding that your behaviors, thoughts, and emotions are linked.

Your behaviors and thoughts can either reduce or ignite your natural emotions. If you desire to shift your emotional condition away from anger, you can alter what you are thinking about and what you are performing.

These strategies consist of shifting away from the behaviors and thought that ignite your angry emotions. With no fuel to keep the fire burning internally, the fire will start to dwindle, and you will calm down finally.

Do some exercises.

Physical exercise can assist minimize the stress that can lead to you getting angry. If you feel that your angry emotion is escalating, take time and go for a brisk run or walk, or spend time practicing other enjoyable physical exercises.

Regular physical exercise assists you to decompress. Aerobic exercise minimizes stress, which might assist in enhancing your frustrations tolerance.

Think before speaking.

In the heat of an outburst, it is very simple to utter something that you may later regret. Always take a few minutes to gather your thought before uttering any word, and often let others who are involved in the situation to do the same.

Once you are calm, express your angry emotions.

When you start thinking in a clearer manner, express your angry emotions in a more assertive but non-confrontational manner. Identify your needs and concerns directly and clearly, without harming anyone.

Recognize the warning signals.

You might feel that anger has hit you in an instant. But, there are warning signs when your angry emotions are on the rise. Identifying those signals can assist you in responding so that you can calm down yourself, relax, and prevent your anger from getting to the raging point.

Often think about the physical signs of anger. Perhaps your heart races fast or your face feels hot or turns red.

Often stick to "I" statements.

For you to avoid placing blame or criticizing; which might only increase tension, it is good if you apply the 'I' statements to explain the problem. Always be specific and respectful. For instance, say, "I am angry that you left the table without offering to assist with the plates" instead of "You never perform and house chores."

Identify possible solutions.

Instead of you concentrating on the cause of your anger, work, or focus on solving the matter at hand.

Always remind yourself that anger will not resolve anything, and it might only make things worse.

Often take time out.

You should realize that timeout are not only for kids. Giving yourself mid breaks during stressful days at work or home will assist you to feel better prepared to deal with what is ahead without getting angry or irritated.

Apply humor to release tension.

A bit of lightening up might assist fade away tension. Apply humor to assist you in dealing with what is getting you upset and any unrealistic expectation. Always avoid sarcasm, though, it can damage emotions and make things worse.

Engage in a physical relaxation exercise.

There are various physical relaxation activities, and it is key to figure out the one exercise that is effective for you. Progressive muscle relaxation and breathing exercise are two popular techniques for minimizing tension.

The appropriate aspect is that both activities can be carried out discreetly and quickly. So whether you are upset at work, you dissolve the tension and stress very fast.

Create a calm-down kit.
If you often come home from work stressed out, and take out your frustrations on your kids and wife, generate a calm down kit that you can apply to calm you down and relax.

Think about things that can assist you to engage your natural senses. If you can touch, hear, smell, and see calming things, you can alter your emotional condition.

You might create a kind of virtual calm-down kit that you carry everywhere—calming images and music, instructions for deep breathing, or guided meditation activities that could be downloaded in a unique folder in your smartphone.

Explore emotions beneath your anger.
It assists in taking time and thinking what feelings may be lurking below your frustrations. Angry emotions

serve as a defensive tool to assist you in avoiding having more painful feelings.

Acknowledging the underlying feelings and labeling them can assist you in getting to the root of the problem. Thereafter you can decide to take the appropriate response.

Progressive Muscle Relaxation

Progressive muscle relaxation (PMR) is an anxiety minimization method invented by an American physician. The method consists of alternating relaxation and tension in all the muscle sets.

If you experience SAD, oftentimes, your muscles are tensed. Practicing this technique, you will understand how a relaxed muscle feels from a tensed muscle set.

PMR is primarily applied along with behavioral therapy tactics like systematic desensitization. However, practicing this method by itself will provide a significant feeling of control over your body's anxiety reaction.

Note that when you carry out this technique perfectly, you may end up falling asleep. If it happens, congratulate and appreciate yourself on attaining such a deep state of relaxation.

How to Practice PMR

Figure out a quiet place that is free from distraction. Recline on a chair or lie on the floor, loosen all the tight attire, and get rid of contacts or glasses. Rest your arms on the chair or rest your hands on your lap. Slowly take a few even breaths. If not, take some few minutes practicing diaphragmatic breathing.

Now, concentrate your attention on the following aspects, being careful to relax the rest of your body parts:

Jaw

Slowly tense the muscle in your jaw for fifteen seconds. Thereafter, release the tension slowly as you count for thirty seconds. You will realize a feeling of relaxation and then continue to breathe evenly and slowly.

Hands and Arms

Slowly draw both of your hands into fists. Pull your fists into your chest and hold gently for fifteen seconds, while you squeeze as tight as you can. Thereafter slowly release as you count for thirty seconds. You will realize the feeling of relaxation.

Forehead

Slowly squeeze the muscles in your forehead, hold for fifteen seconds. Feel the muscles getting tenser and tighter. Thereafter, release the tension in your forehead slowly as you count for thirty seconds. You will realize the difference in how your muscles feel and the sensation of relaxation. Continue to release the tension in your forehead until it feels fully relaxed. Continue breathing evenly and slowly.

Shoulders and Neck

Maximize the tension in your shoulders and neck by raising your shoulders towards your ears and hold there for fifteen seconds. Slowly release the tension as you count for thirty seconds. You will notice the tension fading away.

Legs

Slowly, maximize the tension in the calve and quadriceps over fifteen seconds. Slowly squeeze the muscles as hard as possible. Thereafter, gently release the tension over thirty seconds. You will notice tension fading away, and the feeling of relaxation is left.

Feet

Slowly maximize the tension in your toes and feet. Tighten the muscles as much as you can. Then, slowly release the tension while you count for thirty seconds. You will notice all the tension fading away. Continue breathing evenly and slowly.

Buttocks

Slowly maximize the tension in your buttocks for over fifteen seconds. Then, slowly release the tension for over thirty seconds. You will notice the tension fading away. Continue to breathe evenly and slowly.

Relaxation methods such as PMR can be useful for severe to moderate social anxiety—if practiced together with traditional treatment such as medication or cognitive behavioral therapy.

Breathing Therapy

Breathing activities or exercise provide a simple, convenient, and effective means to reduce stress and reverse stress reaction, minimizing the destructive impacts of severe stress. Simple diaphragm breathing can give your stress relief and relaxation. There are various forms of breathing therapy techniques you can try. But remember each has its twist.

Here are some of the breathing techniques used to keep in check your stress level, thus controlling your anger emotions. Some of the techniques are unique and can each assist in anger and stress management.

Mindful Diaphragmatic Breathing

Allow yourself in a comfortable posture, close your eyes, and begin to realize your breath. Prior to starting to alter your breath: pay close attention to the depth and pace. Are you taking shallow breaths or deep breaths? Are you breathing slowly or fast? Note that you are getting to understand your breathing patterns can assist you to be mindful of your body's reaction to stress and can assist you to realize when you require this deliberately relax your breathing pattern.

Visualization Breathing

Inflating the Balloon

Take a comfortable posture, close your eyes, and start breathing in via your nose and exhale via your mouth. As you inhale, imagine that your abdomen is inflating with air just like a balloon. As you breathe out, just imagine that the air is escaping the balloon slowly.

Note that, you do not have to force that air out; air escapes on its own. You may imagine the balloon as your favorite color and floating high in the sky, with each breath. Regardless, the inflating balloon visualization can assist you to breathe deeply from your diaphragm rather than engaging in shallow breathing that can come from stress.

Releasing Stress

Take a comfortable posture, close your eyes, and begin diaphragmatic breathing. As you inhale, imagine that all the stress in your body is coming out from your extremities and into your chest. Thereafter, as you breathe out, imagine the stress is leaving your body through your breath and dissipating right in front of you. Slowly, deliberately repeat the process. After some breaths, you should feel your stress start to fade away slowly.

Counted Breathing

When you count your breaths, it can be very meaningful, as a form of pacing and meditation. This method assists with pacing; it allows you to elongate your breath and stretch out your breathing out. There are steps to achieve this:

- As you breathe in, place your tongue on the roof of the mouth right behind your teeth, then breathe through your nose and slowly count down from five; on the breathing out, allow the air to escape through your mouth and count back to eight. Thereafter, repeat. This assists you to empty your lungs and relax.

- A variation of this is called 4-7-8 breathing and is highly suggested. With this alternative, you breathe in for a count of four, wait for seven counts, and breathe out for a count of eight. This lets you pause between the breaths and slow things down.

Alternate Nostril Breathing
This breathing technique variation has been carried out for decades as a type of meditative breathing. As you breathe in, put your finger over your right nostril and only breathe through the left nostril. On the breathing

out, shift nostril and only breathe through the right nostril while you block the left nostril. You can breathe at whatever pace that is okay with you, either a 4-7-8 ratio or a 5-8 ratio.

Deep Cleansing Breathing

There are times that you require to release stress from your back, shoulder, and the rest of your body in a few big, cleansing breaths. Inhale deeply through your nose, and breath in as much air as you can. Thereafter release the air, and concentrate on the emptying of your lungs.

Most people hold air in their lungs after breathing out, so emptying your lungs on a deep breath out can assist you in getting more fresh air full of oxygen in the lungs. Repeat this technique for a few breaths and release the tension in your shoulders and your back.

Chapter 8

Meditation Techniques

What Is Meditation?

It is a practice where one tries to concentrate, focus, and train to clear the mind, calm their emotions, or accomplish higher states of consciousness.

Meditation has existed for so long—there are many different form, tactics, and schools of meditation as there are beliefs.

Many people grow up learning how to categorize, compete, compare, and assign decisions and evaluation onto almost everything you encounter. You're especially encouraged to meditate with yourself.

One form of meditation called mindfulness meditation involves staying still and becoming watchful and observant of the thoughts, sensation, and emotions you experience without judgment and from a place of neutrality. When you learn to stay with and observe different emotions and thoughts as they arise, you cannot only become aware of unconscious scripts that you play in your minds but also learn to identify false and negative beliefs about yourself and the universe, as well as become more accepting and compassionate of your own emotions.

How Meditation Alters Thought Pattern

Thought pattern control is very important to a productive and meaningful life. Without thought pattern control, you would be daydreaming for long hours and be in endless problems of responding to fleeting irrational thoughts.

Because your brain is very complex, both children and adults usually have a challenge in concentrating their focus on only one person or task. With the aid of meditation, however, most people can learn and understand how to better control their thought processes and enhance their focus.

Your brain continuously processes information that it gets from your ears, eyes, and the other sensory organs. For instance, when you hear a car drive by while you are typing a document, your brain records the sound of the car's engine and links it to your memory for identifying. Recognition of the source of sound allows your body and mind know that you are safe to proceed to type, but then before you realize it, you are thinking about a past event associated to cars instead of the work at hand.

Random memories and thoughts lead to these lapses in concentration, particularly when stimulated with intense emotion.

In such an instance, an inability to control your thought can lead to poor decision making.

Meditation lets you manage the direction of your thought process, including the one that generates adverse emotional reactions.

As you concentrate during a meditation activity, your mind figures out a tranquil place where you can focus despite having random thoughts. This creates a feeling of serenity that you wouldn't consciously face on the outside universe. You can learn and understand to induce the meditative condition in your daily routine. Once you develop a habit to concentrate on the current and your stillness, you are better prepared to neglect the random thoughts that would interrupt your meditation.

Not only does meditation techniques provide you with mind control capabilities, but it also assists you to concentrate on possible alternatives, positivity, and the achievement of your future and present goals.

Meditation Enhances Key Brain Regions

Deep meditation enhances or upgrades vital brain regions. Meditation has so many benefits:

- More happiness
- Change your brain, change your life
- Better memory
- Deeper sleep
- Less stress
- More success
- Higher EQ and IQ
- Easier learning

Life Extension and Longevity

Meditators usually look so young than their real age, but also live a much longer life. Here, you take a glimpse at the fascinating age-defying studies making headlines, and how meditation practices freeze further time.

Subconscious Mind Power

Your unconscious and subconscious mind are very powerful. You will learn and understand the vast benefits, and how meditation is the perfect means to dive in, harness, and explore your inner mind.

Weight Loss

Have you ever asked yourself why meditators are usually trim and slim? It is because weight loss is one of the advantages of meditation is perfect. Meditation techniques can propel you to your ideal body size.

Entire Body Synchronization

Meditation balances your right and left brain hemispheres, resulting in what is known as the entire brain synchronization. This opens the door to several amazing benefits. This include:

- Perfect mental health

- Easier and faster learning

- Super creativity

Meditation Techniques Applied for Anger

Guided Meditation

In spite of the various advantages of meditation, most people feel more overwhelmed at the thought of how to practice meditation. Guided meditation makes it easier to get started because it takes various mental legwork away from the novice.

It allows you to be guided by another person. A guide that may assist you in drumming up some particular mental imagery, or they may walk you through a process of mantras or breathing exercise to assist you in learning and practicing meditation for anger relief.

When you are able to find the guided meditation in the form of a video, an in-studio or even podcast, a guide can assist you to meditate in a step by step approach. Thereafter, you can focus on meditating and relaxing, rather than worrying about the form or technique.

Getting a Guide

Although the digital universe makes it hard to disconnect, it does not have its perks; it is easier than ever to get a guided meditation on demand. For you to find the perfect meditation guide practice for you, go through some of the following options:

- Yoga studios – If you would like to have a taste of the guided meditation practice surrounded by others, search into a yoga studio, that may have classes designed solely to this practice.

- Apps – A study in 2018 published in Cognitive and behavioral practice found out that apps can be very important for mental health. Researchers cautioned users that the most common apps might not primarily provide the most advantage. So while it is probably possible that guided meditation apps can assist you in harnessing the benefits of meditation, do not ignore the most common apps, which are very beneficial. It may take some trial and error a bit of researching on your end to figure out the one that is best for you.

- Podcast – Whether you desire to learn and understand more about meditation or find a fifteen-minute guide, some podcast gives practice and learning opportunities.

- Video websites and YouTube – If you would be interested in visual how other people practice meditation, you might like a video demonstration. Guided meditation videos on YouTube might be of great assistance to you.

- Mindfulness websites – Just a little search engine will bring up a great number of websites that provide free guided meditation in both visual and audio formats.

- Online music services – A subscription to a streaming music service, for example, Apple Music, or Spotify gives you access to many guided meditation sessions that range in feeling and length.

Set a Time to Meditate

It is much easier for you to fall into the trap of practicing meditation later, but later never really comes. If you are sincerely interested in meditation, it's very important for you to set a particular time in your routine for meditation.

Most people will consider either the first thing in the morning or the last thing in the evening before they retire to bed. These are viable time to practice meditation. This is because these are the quietest time of the day.

A single perk to performing meditation in the early morning is that it begins your day off on the right foot and that means that you do not have to attempt to create time to fit in between work, chores or meetings. Contrary, meditating right before you go to bed can get you into a state of relaxation that is just perfect for a sound sleep.

Getting the Most Out of a Guided Meditation

Once you have decided to begin a meditation activity, begin by turning your phone on airplane or silent mode. Take a short break from being connected for five to ten minutes during this period. Free from distraction will help you to harness the most from a meditation exercise.

Then, lie somewhere comfortable. This could be on a cushion that has been set on the far corner of your favorite room or your bed. Close your eyes, breathe naturally, and allow the guide to take it from there.

In order to make meditation a regular exercise, you might find that you require to put meditation time into your daily schedule. Make meditation a regular habit at a particular time of the day, and you are likely to find that you will be committed to meditation more regularly.

Note that meditation takes practice. No one is necessarily perfect at meditation at first. It takes dedication and practice to reap the benefits.

The Process of Meditating

Meditation novices often find the process of meditating to be almost mentally not comfortable at the start. The mind is bound to wonder at the start, even when you are guided.

It is natural to get lost in your thoughts, and it is not necessarily the aim of meditation to stop thinking completely or to empty the mind. It is about paying close attention to your body.

When this occurs, pause to consider what you were thinking about and why it was distracting you. Thereafter, let it go and return your awareness to your breath and how your body responds to each exhale and inhale.

As you continue your practice, keeping your mind focused will be much easier. Note that there is no wrong way to practice meditation, even when it is a guided meditation. It is supposed to be about what feels good to you.

When the guided part of your mediation ends, do not jump back into the hectic pace of your daily routine. Allow yourself to end the mediation slowly and remain present at the moment.

Gradually become reawakened to the universe around you and slowly open your eyes. Return to the daily routine with the renewed clear and invigorating mind.

Types of Meditation Techniques

This is a widely recommended way to manage stress and for a good purpose. Meditation offers several mental enhancing benefits, like:

- Improving your immune system

- Relieving physical complaints such as headache

- Reducing symptoms of anxiety and stress

Basics of Meditation

It can be carried out in various means. While there are many varieties of meditation techniques, a popular thread runs through virtually all meditative tactics. These include:

- Be in the know – Rather than concentrating on the future or the past, basically every meditative practice consists of concentrating on the right now. Right Now, involves facing each particular event and letting it go, then you face the next moment. It also takes practice to achieve this, as most of you live mostly thinking about the future or rehashing the past.

- Altered state – With time, maintaining a silent mind and concentration on the current moment can cause an altered state of consciousness that is not a sleeping state, but it is quite the average of a wakeful state. Meditation practice maximizes the mind activity in the aspect of the mind relating to positive thoughts, happiness, and emotions, and some evidence shows that regular meditation practice brings a prolonged positive change in these aspects.

- A quiet mind – When practicing meditation, the thinking process becomes quiet. You stop concentrating on the stressors of your daily routine's problem, as well as resolving the problems. Just allow that voice in your head to be quiet, that is easier said than done.

Meditation techniques are classified under two categories non-concentrative and concentrative. Concentrative consists of concentrating on a specific object that is generally outside oneself. Non-concentrative include a broader focus; the voices in your environment as well as your inner body state and your breathing aspects. These techniques include:

1. Focused meditation technique – Your concentration is on something intently, but do not involve your thoughts about the process. You can concentrate on something visually, like a statue; something auditory, like a metronome, something that is constant, like your breathing pace. Most people find it easier to perform this than to concentrate on nothing, but the concept is the same; remaining in the present situation and circumventing the constant stream of commentary from your conscious mind and letting yourself to shift into an altered condition of consciousness.

2. Mindfulness technique – This can be a type of meditation that, like activity-oriented, does not seem like meditation. It just involves remaining in the present situation rather than thinking about the past or the future. Concentrating on the sensation that you feel in your body is one technique to remain in the current moment; concentrating on emotions and where you feel them in your body is another.

3. Basic meditation technique – This form of meditation consists of sitting in a more comfortable posture and trying to silence your mind by thinking of nothing. It is not often easy to perform this if you do not have constant practice. But a good technique to start is to think of yourself as an observer of your thoughts, just noticing what the narrative voice in your head is saying, but not interacting with the voice. As the thoughts materialize in the brain, allow the thoughts to go. That is the basic concept.

4. Activity-oriented – This is a type of mindfulness that primarily bundles meditation with activities you like, that assist you to concentrate on the current situation. With the form of meditation, you participate in a repetitive activity where you can get in the experience flow. This silences your brain and lets your mind to shift. Activities such as practicing yoga, gardening, and artwork can be forms of meditation.

5. Spiritual meditation – Most people face meditation as a type of prayer session; the type where God literally communicates rather than just listening. That is correct—most people experience inner wisdom or guidance once the brain is silent, and meditate for this reason. You can meditate on a single question until a response comes, or meditate to clear their brain and agree to whatever that comes that day.

Chapter 9

Personality Disorder

This is a form of mental illness in which you possess an unhealthy and rigid pattern of operating, behaving, and the thought process. Someone with this personality disorder has difficulty in associating and perceiving to people and situation. This leads to larger problems and difficulties in work, social activities, school, and relationships.

In some instances, you might not notice that you possess a personality disorder because your manner of behaving and thinking seems very natural to yourself—and you might blame other people for the difficulties you are facing.

Personality disorder often starts in these teenage years. There are several forms of personality disorder. Some forms might get less obvious throughout the middle age.

Paranoid Personality Disorder (PDD)

PDD forms a group of conditions known as eccentric personality disorders or Cluster A. A person with PDD suffer from paranoia, an unrelenting suspicion, and mistrust of other people, even when there is no purpose of being suspicious.

People with this personality disorder usually appear peculiar or odd. The necessary characteristic of a person with PDD is a relentless suspicion of another person without enough purpose to be suspicious. This disorder usually starts in early adolescence or childhood and manifest to be more popular in men than in women.

Causes

A particular cause of PDD is unknown, but it is likely to be involved in a combination of psychological and biological factors. The fact that PDD is popular in people who have first degree relatives with delusional and schizophrenia disorder suggests a genetic relation between the two illness. It is believed that early childhood experiences, including emotional or physical trauma, play a part in the advancement of PDD.

Symptoms of PDD

Those suffering from PDD are often on alert, believing that other people are constantly attempting to demean, threaten, or harm them. These unfounded beliefs, as well as their behaviors of distrust and blame, disrupt with their ability to create close or even workable relationship.

People with this paranoid personality disorder:

- Have challenges in relaxing

- Tend to develop negative stereotypes of other people, specifically those from various cultural groups

- Are argumentative, hostile and stubborn

- Are primarily distant and cold in their close relationships and may get jealous and controlling for the avoidance of being betrayed

- Can't see their role in conflict or problems, believing they are often right

- Have a persistent suspicion, without any reason, that their lovers or spouses are not faithful

- They are unforgiving and hold grudges

- They take criticism poorly and are hypersensitive

- Doubt the trustworthiness, commitment, or loyalty of other people, believing other people are deceiving or exploiting them.

- They are reluctant to confide in others because they are afraid the information will be used against them

Schizoid Personality Disorder

In this type of condition, a person avoids social events and consistently keep away from interacting with other people. They also have a limited variety of emotional expression.

If you have this disorder, you may be viewed as dismissive of others or loner, and you may lack the skill or urge to form a close personal relationship.

Causes of Schizoid Personality Disorder

Less is known about the root cause of this type of disorder, but both environment and genetics are suggested to play a role. Various mental health professionals suggest that a bleak childhood upbringing where emotion and warmth were absent plays a role in the advancement of this illness. The higher the probability of this illness in families of schizophrenics speculates that a genetic susceptibility for the illness might be inherited.

Symptoms

People with this disorder usually are reclusive, organizing their lifestyle to avoid contact with other people. Most of them never marry or try to continue to live with their guardians as adults. Other common traits include the following:

- They show little emotion and stay aloof.

- They have difficulties relating to other people.

- They daydream.

- They are indifferent to criticism or praise.

- They have no close allies, except close relatives.

- They prefer solitary activities and jobs.

- They do not enjoy a close relationship even with friends or family members.

Treatment

People who suffer from this disorder rarely seek medical attention because their behavior and thoughts do not lead to distress. If treatment is sought, psychotherapy; this is a form of counseling. The therapy is likely to concentrate on increasing coping techniques, as well as on enhancing self-esteem, communication, and social interaction. Since trust is a vital element of therapy, treatment can be hard for the therapist because people suffering from this disorder have challenges in building relationships with other people. Social skills training can also be a vital element of treatment.

Schizophrenia Personality Disorder

This is a severe, severe mental illness that impacts the way a person relates to others, perceives reality, thinks, acts, and expresses feelings to other people. Though it is not very popular as other mental disorders, it can be the most disabling and chronic.

People with this personality disorder usually have problems doing well in the community, relationship, at school, and work. They may feel frightened, withdrawn, and could seem to have lost touch with reality.

Early Symptoms of Schizophrenia Personality Disorder

This condition often shows its first early signs in men in their early twenties. Schizophrenia affects women in their early thirties and twenties. The period when symptoms first begin and prior to full psychosis is known as the prodromal period.

You may notice a subtle behavioral change, particularly in teens. This include:

- Temper flares

- Social withdrawal

- Difficulty sleeping

- Trouble focusing

- A change in performance or grade

Positive Symptoms

In this context, positively does not refer to good. Positive refers to added actions or thoughts that are not tied in reality. They are sometimes known as psychotic symptoms. This include:

1. Hallucinations. It involves a sensation that is not actual. Hearing voices is the most popular hallucination in people suffering from schizophrenia.

2. Catatonia. At this stage, the person may stop speaking, and their body might be fixed in one position for a long time.

3. Delusions. Delusions are mixed, false, and strange beliefs that are not tied to reality and that the patient refuses to give up, even when shown the truth.

Cognitive Symptoms

The person will have trouble:

- Recognizing that they have any of these problems

- Paying attention or focusing

- Applying their information instantly after learning

- Understanding information and applying the information to make decisions.

Negative Symptoms

Absence of normal, natural behaviors in people with this disorder. Negative symptoms include:

- Lack of motivation

- Poor grooming habits and hygiene

- Loss of interest in life

- Less energy

- Speaking less

- Limited range of emotions or lack of emotion

- Withdrawal from social activities, family and friends

Causes of Schizophrenia Personality Disorder

1. Environment – Factors like viral infections, being exposed to toxins like marijuana, or stressful events may stimulate schizophrenia in people whose genes make them prone to the illness.

2. Brain circuits and chemistry – Those suffering from this personality disorder may not have the ability to control brain chemicals called neurotransmitter that is responsible for controlling particular pathways of nerve cells that impact behavior and thinking

3. Genetics – Schizophrenia runs in families' genes. That means a significant likelihood to

suffer from the disorder. It may be passed on from a parent to the kid.

4. Brain abnormality – Studies have discovered abnormal brain structure in people with schizophrenia. But it does not apply to every person suffering from schizophrenia. It can also affect people without the disorder.

How Is Schizophrenia Diagnosed?

A person is diagnosed with this disorder if he/she has at least two of the following symptoms for at least six months:

- Negative symptoms
- Hallucination
- Disorganized speech
- Delusions
- Disorganized behavior

Antisocial Personality Disorder (ASPD)

People suffering ASPD can be fun, witty, and charming to be close to, but they also lie and exploit other people.

ASPD makes people uncaring. A person with this personality illness may respond destructively, unsafely, and rashly without feeling guilty when their actions harm others.

Modern diagnostic methods consider antisocial personality disorder to involve two associated conditions: A psychopath is a person whose harmful reactions towards other people reflect cunning, manipulation and calculation; they feel no empathy or emotion for other people. These people can be deceptively charming and charismatic. Contrary, sociopaths are able to form attachments to other people but still they disregard social rules; these people are easily agitated, more haphazard, and impulsive than others with psychopathy.

Symptoms
People with this disorder may usually do the following:

- Fail to meet their social duties

- Break law

- Abuse drugs or alcohol

- They do not show any signs of remorse after harming someone

- They do not care about the safety of others

- They act harshly

- Assault or fight others

- Be aggressive, angry and vain

- Exploit, con, or lie to others

Who Is at Risk?

ASPD affects more men than women. Medical experts do not understand for sure what causes ASPD, but biological factors and genetics are suggested to play a part in its development—growing up in an abusive environment, particularly for sociopathy. Brain injuries and defects during developmental years may also be associated with ASPD.

Borderline Personality Disorder (BPD)

This is a severe mental disorder. It often starts in the early 20s or late teens. Women are more affected by this disorder compared to men.

There is an unknown cause, but it is assumed to be a combination of the way the brain is structured and the things a person experience during their upbringing.

For instance, you may be prone to suffer from this disorder based on the genes passed down through your family lineage. But then, something might occur that can stimulate it, such as being neglected or abused.

If you are suffering from a borderline personality disorder, you may have difficulties in controlling and managing your emotions. This may cause you to:

- Have a fit of anxiety, depression, or anger

- Take unnecessary risk

- Have intense mood swings

You may find it challenging to:

- Excel at work

- Maintain an intimate relationship

- Manage daily routine at home

This may lead to things like separation of friends and family or even divorce, and severe financial problems.

Borderline personality disorder is not an isolated problem. If you have this personality disorder, you are more likely to have another mental issue, such as thoughts of suicide, anxiety, eating disorder, and depression. Most people turn to alcohol and drugs, which can bring more problems for you.

Chapter 10

Understanding Your Anxiety

Anxiety

Disproportionate responses of worry and tension do characterize anxiety.

Anxiety is a natural feeling characterized by emotions of worrying thought, as well as physical changes such as increased tension and blood pressure.

Understanding the differences between normal emotions and anxiety and anxiety illness that needs urgent medical attention can assist someone in identifying and managing the disorder.

Anxiety is a natural and usually healthy feeling. However, when someone regularly experiences disproportionate amounts of anxiety, this might become a medical disorder.

Anxiety illness forms a group of mental health diagnoses that cause excessive worry, fear, nervousness, and apprehension.

When Anxiety Requires Treatment

While anxiety might lead to distress, anxiety is not often a medical condition.

When a person experience potential worrying or harmful feelings and triggers of anxiety are normal but essential for survival.

Since evolution, the procedure of incoming danger and predators set off triggers in the body and let evasive or attack response. These triggers become noticeable in the form of a raised heartbeat, increased sensitivity, and profuse sweating.

The danger leads to a rush release of adrenalin, a chemical messenger in mind, which in turn stimulates these anxious reactions.

Most people, running from imminent harm is a less urgent concern than it would have been for early beings. Anxieties now operate around health, work, family life, money, and other important matters that require a person's close attention without essential requiring to flight or fight response.

The feeling of being nervous before a crucial life situation or in a challenging event is a natural reaction of the natural flight or fight response. It is still important to survival.

Anxiety Disorders

The period of the severity of an anxious emotion can disproportionate to the original stressor or trigger. Physical signs or symptoms, such as nausea and increased blood pressure, may be seen. These reactions move above the normal, natural anxiety into an anxiety disorder.

A person with an anxiety disorder has recurring intrusive concerns or thoughts. Once anxiety is at the state of a disorder, it can affect your daily routine.

Symptoms of Anxiety Disorder

Different diagnoses constitute anxiety disorder, and the symptoms of the generalized disorder will usually include the following:

- Difficulties in concentrating

- Difficulties in sleeping

- The uncontrollable feeling of worry

- Increased irritability

- Restlessness

People with a generalized anxiety disorder will experience these symptoms to extreme or persistent levels. A general anxiety disorder may manifest as vague, unsettling worry, or chronic anxiety that interferes with the daily routine.

Types of Anxiety Disorder

Panic Disorder

Sudden or brief attacks of severe apprehension and terror characterize the panic disorder. Panic attacks cause nausea, breathing problems, confusion, dizziness, and shaking. The attacks happen and escalate very fast, peaking after ten minutes. An attack might take up to several hours.

Symptoms
An attack usually emanates from a direct incident or trigger, but the attacks can start randomly and

suddenly with no clear cause. Panic attacks are assumed to emanate from an evolutionary reaction to harm.

Having these attacks is said to be intensely uncomfortable, frightening, and upsetting situations in a person's life.

A panic attack involves at least four of the below symptoms:

- Breathing problems, feeling smothering
- Tingling or numbness
- Sweating
- Trembling or shaking
- Feelings of choking
- Stomach upset and nausea
- Rapid heart rate, heart palpitations, or irregular heartbeat
- Feeling lightheaded or dizziness
- Experiencing a sudden intense fear of dying

- Discomfort and chest pain

- Feeling unusual hot and chills

An attack can also be linked with agoraphobia, a fear of places where the patient assumes to be harmful and hard to escape from. A person who has experienced an attack usually say after that they felt trapped.

Causes of Panic Disorder
Panic and anxiety, to a particular extent, are an essential part of your survival instinct. However, when the levels of anxiety and panic get high that they impact the rational thought process negatively, a person normally gets afraid.

When your brain gets a surge of nervous signals created to warn you of potential harm, the amygdala, is stimulated. Amygdala regulates a person's anxious reaction.

Some people's amygdala responds to anxiety when there is no potential harm, making it that they will experience frequent panic attacks and high levels of anxiety.

When you receive a signal to respond to anxiety, your body will generate adrenaline, also called epinephrine.

A release of the chemical to the body raises the heartbeat, provoke irregular breathing, churn the stomach, and cause profuse sweating.

If there is no imminent danger and the body is full of adrenalin, adrenalin will not be used. The build-up of adrenalin in a person body can lead to a panic attack.

Some risk factors can maximize the probability of a person having a panic disorder and a panic attack:

- Genetics may play a part – If someone has a close relative, like a sibling or a parent with panic disorder; they may be more prone to suffer a panic attack.

- Family history – Experiencing major life changes or stressful events can stimulate increased panic attacks and anxiety

- Behaviors such as drinking excessive alcohol or large amounts of caffeine or smoking are also risk factors related to panic attacks.

Treatment

Most common treatments are psychotherapy and medications.

Talk therapy involves talking with a qualified licensed mental health professional to help identify potential triggers of a panic attack in the purpose of getting over fears.

Prevention

For panic attacks, some lifestyles changes can assist a person to minimize the occurrence of panic disorder and panic attacks.

Examples include:

- Getting sufficient sleep every night

- Taking appropriate steps to minimize stress in your life, such as participating in regular physical activities, practicing yoga, and engaging in deep breathing

- Joining a support group, if you experience the panic attacks frequently

- Avoiding substances that trigger panic attack such as smoking l, excessive caffeine, or using recreational drugs

Social Anxiety Disorder

Social anxiety disorder is also called social phobia. A phobia is an irrational fear of a particular environment, situation, or object.

Social anxiety disorder can involve a fear of being judged by other people.

Someone with social phobia may be very fearful of embarrassment in social events. This fear can affect the professional and personal relationship.

Social phobia usually happens early in childhood as a normal part of social development and may go unnoticed until the person is mature enough. The triggers and frequency of social phobia vary depending on the person.

Most people feel nervous in particular social events, such as taking part in a competition. It is normal and would not qualify as a social anxiety disorder.

Quick Facts about Social Anxiety

- Treatment can involve medication and psychotherapy.

- Those with social anxiety are disproportionately nervous in social events.

- Social anxiety disorder is popular in women than in men.

Symptoms of Social Anxiety Disorder
They may be behavioral, physical, or emotional symptoms. Social anxiety disorder can influence your daily tasks, including work and education.

Emotional and behavioral symptoms include:

- A blank mind during social events that cause anxiety

- Fear of meeting people in power or authority

- Panic attacks or severe anxiety when facing the feared event

- Excessive fear of embarrassment

- Fear of being in events with strangers

- Dread concerning how he/she will be introduced to other people

- Avoiding events where the person feels that he/she may be the center of attention

Physical symptoms and signs include:

1. Dry throat and mouth

2. Trembling and shaking

3. Muscle tension

4. Nausea

5. Excessive sweating

6. Cold hands and clammy

7. Avoiding eye contact

8. Abdominal pain

9. Blushing

10. Heart palpitations

A person experiencing social anxiety disorder may also:

- Be not assertive

- Have poor social skills

- Have a low self-esteem

- They talk negatively about self, with self-defeating and inaccurate thoughts

- Be oversensitive to criticism

Here are the causes of social anxiety disorder:

- Chemicals in the body system

  Currently, scientists are researching which chemical components in the body might enhance the advancement of social anxiety disorder. Serotonin, a brain chemical may play a major role when the amounts are not high. A person is compassionate.

- Demographics and weather

Countries in the Mediterranean have low rates of this disorder compared to the Scandinavian countries. This could be a fact, because of the hot weather as well as the high population. The warm environment may minimize the avoidance of social situation and maximize contact with other people.

- Genetics

  The condition seems to run in families. Hence it could be inherited from one person to a close relative.

Overcoming Anxiety

Triggering positive thoughts before a potentially intimidating social interaction, such as listening to the music you love, this will assist you in nurturing positive emotions during the encounter.

One factor that makes symptoms of SAD worse is the fear of becoming anxious itself.

The more anxious someone feels about social events, the less likely it is they will expose themselves to the social event.

Being more exposed to social events, however, it is important to get over anxiety, and the less an individual expose themselves to social events, the more severe the anxiety gets.

It is very vital to break the series of anxious thought. These are steps proven to assist in preparing a person for a social event that may feel nervous prior to having them. These include:

- Stimulating positive thought prior to social interactions

- Reframing negative thought process

- Not depending on narcotics or alcohol

Treatment

It is a lifelong disorder for most people, often altering in how extreme it is. Various treatments can be used to assist a person to control their symptoms and gain confidence.

Psychotherapy

This a psychological treatment that applies to a variety of tactics to assist the patient in seeing themselves and their issues in a realistic light and easy to cope and overcome with them effectively.

Cognitive Behavioral Therapy (CBT)

Cognitive behavioral therapy assists the person to notice that it is their thoughts, rather than other people's thought, that will determine how they respond or respond. In this aspect of psychotherapy, the person learns and understand how to recognize and alter negative thoughts about themselves.

CBT has two main parts, namely:

- A behavioral aspect, created to change the manner in which a person responds to events or objects that trigger anxiety

- A cognitive component, created to limit disproportionate or distorted thinking.

The person also receives exposure therapy, that they gradually work up to facing the situation they fear.

With cognitive delivered exposure, the person safely confronts the events that cause the disorder, usually in the company of a therapist.

Conclusion

Each one of you faces anger in different ways, and so, you require to learn to manage your anger in the manner that perfectly works for you. Once you have identified the form of anger that you face often, you can begin the process to controlling and managing your angry emotions in a constructive way that allows you to convert your angry emotions from a destructive tool into a powerful friend. Note that that process to anger-free life may need some professional help. It should never be viewed as a sign of weakness—a person should be admired for facing up and dealing with their challenges and taking active measure to eliminate angry emotions.

Emotions are normally temporary. Allow yourself to feel your feelings, and the emotions will pass. Anger management needs paying close attention to the things that you require—not ignoring the necessity or the emotion. Anger does signal you to pay close attention—

something is not quite okay. It is never weak or wrong to express emotions despite what some of you heard and made to believe when they were toddlers.

Recognizing the impacts of unchecked anger can give you the motivation to alter it. Attempt to pinpoint the signs and symptoms of anger early enough so that you can express it without harming others or yourself. You will be glad that you did that.

It is very vital to recognize that the impacts of angry emotions can either be negative or positive. When unchecked angry emotions reach the optimum level, and it motivates you to leave an abusive relationship or abusive partner, your angry emotions have saved you from more abuse. Contrary, if you apply your angry emotions to frighten other people into performing what you desire them to do without considering their desires, you are letting your angry emotions to control and force other people, and you are not better than a bully.

There are many forms that angry emotions can take, but those discussed above are the most common that is faced by many people. Management of anger is a fascinating aspect of research—there is a strong context of evidence that the practical techniques discussed above are effective techniques for regulating angry emotions, behavior, and thoughts.

Made in the USA
Middletown, DE
26 December 2019